way, Massachusetts, 2002 ◆ Marian Fathers Ballfields, Chicago, 2003 ◆ Elkhorn Ranch, Utah, 2004 ◆ ...

...◆ Rum River, Minnesota, 2010 ◆ Walden Woods, Massachusetts, 1991-1994 ◆ Gallatin County ...

...tional Wildlife Refuge, Florida, 1976 ◆ Lindbergh Lake, Montana, 2000 ◆ Chief Joseph Ranch, Oregon, 1999 ◆ Sawtooth

... Park, San Francisco, 1974 ◆ Los Angeles State Historic Park, 2001 ◆ Clinton Community Garden, New York, 1985 ◆ Olympic

...Cuyahoga Valley National Park, Ohio, 1978–2011 ◆ Signal Bay Park, Texas, 1989 ◆ Buffalo Hill Farm, Massachusetts,

...en Gate Canyon State Park, Colorado, 1989 ◆ Gwynns Falls Trail, Baltimore, 1992–2005 ◆ Ruffner Mountain, Alabama,

...d, Harlem, 2006 ◆ Peace River Park, Florida, 1978 ◆ Central Texas Greenprint, 2009 ◆ Dog Mountain, Washington, 1985 ◆

...o Nature Sanctuary, Saint Paul, 2007–2008 ◆ Broad Canyon Ranch, New Mexico, 2009 ◆ Bluebird Ranch, California,

...O'Melveny Park, Los Angeles, 1973 ◆ Mallows Bay, Maryland, 2002 ◆ Cahuenga Peak, Los Angeles, 2012 ◆ Ash Lake,

...untains County Park, New Jersey, 1989 ◆ Gray's Harbor County Park, Washington, 1986 ◆ York River State Park,

...es, Colorado, 2012 ◆ National Bison Range, Montana, 1987 ◆ Overtown Playground, Miami, 2002 ◆ Phillips Farm,

...ey, 1983–2012 ◆ Oakland Bay, Washington, 2012 ◆ Bear Creek Canyon, Colorado, 1992 ◆ Potso Dog Park, Oregon,

...lifornia, 2011 ◆ East River Greenprint, New York, 2003 ◆ Point Lookout State Park, Maryland, 1992 ◆ Nassau County

...Washington, 1987 ◆ Santa Venetia County Park, California, 1974 ◆ Westside Community Garden, New York, 1989 ◆

..., New Hampshire, 1991 ◆ Pine Avenue Park, Los Angeles, 2011 ◆ Weir Farm National Historic Site, Connecticut,

...3 ◆ Katy Prairie, Texas, 1997 ◆ Franklin D. Roosevelt National Historic Site, New York, 1989 ◆ General Morris Forest,

...◆ Thompson Island, Massachusetts, 2002 ◆ Mountain Island Lake, North Carolina, 1998–2009 ◆ Otterbrook, New

...gewood Horse Farm, New Jersey, 2004 ◆ Shadow Lake, New York, 2004 ◆ Wilkins Ranch, California, 1973 ◆ Lake

...n, Ohio, 1982 ◆ Gerard Woods, New Jersey, 2004 ◆ Long Island, Minnesota, 2007 ◆ Arrowhead Farm, Massachusetts,

... 1987 ◆ Weehawken Reservoir, New Jersey, 2001 ◆ Oregon Caves, Oregon, 1979 ◆ Jug Bay Farm, Maryland, 2004 ◆

...d, Michigan, 1990 ◆ Prospect Hill, Massachusetts, 1995 ◆ Dog Creek Falls, Washington, 1985 ◆ Wonder Lake, New

...1 ◆ Lumahai Beach, Hawaii, 2001 ◆ Grace Marchant Garden, San Francisco, 1986 ◆ Knobs State Forest, Kentucky,

...onnecticut, 2004 ◆ Potrero Hill Playground, San Francisco, 2007 ◆ Royal River Estuary, Maine, 2004 ◆ Minneapolis

...on, 1988 ◆ Kirkwood Forest, New Jersey, 2005 ◆ Taxter Ridge, New York, 2004 ◆ Cove Hollow Farm, New York, 1993

...ain, Washington, 1987 ◆ Six Mile Creek, Montana, 1988 ◆ Foster Farm, New York, 1995 ◆ Rocky Creek, Texas, 1994

...ing Bay, Maryland, 1996 ◆ Comanche Lookout, Texas, 1994 ◆ Jewell Wetlands, Colorado, 1995 ◆ Hillside Woods,

New York, 1993 ♦ Cathedral of Pines, Wisconsin, 1990 ♦ Scituate Waterfront Park, Massachusetts, 2004 ♦ Cox Farm, New York, 2005 ♦ Jackman Farm, Connecticut, 1994 ♦ Summer Creek, Oregon, 2010 ♦ Forges Field, Massachusetts, 1993 ♦ Hall Ranch, Colorado, 1996 ♦ Buzzard Rock, West Virginia, 1992 ♦ Andrusia Lake, Minnesota, 1990 ♦ Caspar Headlands, California, 2000 ♦ Spencer Farm, Rhode Island, 1992 ♦ Lawton Park, Washington, 1996 ♦ Monticello Fields, Ohio, 1991 ♦ Olmstead View, Oregon, 1998 ♦ Portland Waterfront, Maine, 1993 ♦ Massacre Marsh, New Hampshire, 2004 ♦ Murray Forest, Connecticut, 1994 ♦ Catamount Ranch, Colorado, 1996 ♦ Witch Hollow Farm, Massachusetts, 1995 ♦ Rush Island, Minnesota, 1991 ♦ McKay Park, Oregon, 2011 ♦ Porter Ranch, California, 2000 ♦ Signal Hill, New Jersey, 2005 ♦ Tierra de Oportunidades, Massachusetts, 2005 ♦ Dagnon Ranch, Washington, 2010 ♦ Homer Spit, Alaska, 1998 ♦ Rye Creek, Montana, 2005 ♦ Big Lake, Washington, 2003 ♦ Black Hole Hollow Farm, Vermont, 1996 ♦ Lake Ottawa, Minnesota, 1991 ♦ St. Clair Buffer, Florida, 2004 ♦ Salt River, Virgin Islands, 2004 ♦ Badger Mountain, Washington, 2005 ♦ Biddle Butte, Washington, 1988 ♦ Senka Park, Chicago, 1991 ♦ Devil's Canyon Ranch, Wyoming, 2003 ♦ Northwoods Scout Reservation, Michigan, 1991 ♦ Ghost Lake, Wisconsin, 1992 ♦ Three Rivers, Arkansas, 2003 ♦ Snow Mountain Ranch, Washington, 2005 ♦ Gilgal Gardens, Utah, 2000 ♦ Jim Creek, Washington, 2010 ♦ Hammonasset River, Connecticut, 1993 ♦ Whalen Island, Oregon, 2000 ♦ Cowling Creek, Washington, 2003 ♦ Moffitt Hollow, Vermont, 1993 ♦ Caribbean Gardens, Florida, 2005 ♦ Glen House, New Hampshire, 1993 ♦ Marquam Woods, Oregon, 1996 ♦ Pocantico Lake, New York, 1992 ♦ Long's Landing, Florida, 2008 ♦ Laidlaw, Oregon, 2008 ♦ Montana Legacy, 1997–2010 ♦ Phelps Creek, Washington, 1997 ♦ Hall Ranch, Colorado, 1996 ♦ South Beach Wetlands, New York, 2006 ♦ Buffalo Lake, Wisconsin, 1992 ♦ Peach Island, Connecticut, 2005 ♦ Reeds Creek Farm, Illinois, 1993 ♦ Halifax River Park, Florida, 2009 ♦ Lake of the Woods, Michigan, 1993 ♦ Estate Maho Bay, Virgin Islands, 2010 ♦ Palmer House, Connecticut, 1994 ♦ Raspberry Farm, New Hampshire, 2009 ♦ Sipican Harbor, Massachusetts, 1996 ♦ Duck Creek Wetlands, Montana, 2004 ♦ Sugarloaf Key, Florida, 2006 ♦ Romine Ranch, Idaho, 2004 ♦ Eldorado Canyon, Colorado, 1985 ♦ Hardwood Ridge, New Hampshire, 2005 ♦ Windrush Farm, Massachusetts, 2009 ♦ Gold Star Farm, New Hampshire, 2005 ♦ Bull Creek Fish Camp, Florida, 2007 ♦ Dorsey Creek, Alabama, 2007 ♦ Boltz Ranch, Montana, 2010 ♦ Agency Lake, Oregon, 1998 ♦ Clark Ranch, California, 2001 ♦ Awosting Preserve, New York, 2006 ♦ Mt. Gilboa, Massachusetts, 1990 ♦ Meserve Farm, Maine, 2004 ♦ Howe Farm, Washington, 1995 ♦ Willamette Cove, Oregon, 1996 ♦ Cumberland Gap, Tennessee, 2007 ♦

Land *for* People

Land *for* People

THE TRUST FOR PUBLIC LAND
and the Future of Conservation

Foreword by Timothy Egan

Edited by William Poole
Text by Diana Landau

THE
TRUST
for
PUBLIC
LAND

Published by The Trust for Public Land
101 Montgomery Street, Suite 900
San Francisco, CA 94104
tpl.org

The Trust for Public Land, TPL, *Land&People*, Conserving Land for People, LandVote, LandLink, Greenprint for Growth, Fitness Zones, and the Trust for Public Land and LandVote logos are registered trademarks of The Trust for Public Land. ParkScore is a trademark of The Trust for Public Land.

Copyright to all photographs in this book is held by the photographer credited or by The Trust for Public Land. All rights reserved.

Front-of-book photographs:
Page 1. Widgeon Point, Beaufort County, South Carolina. *Darcy Kiefel.*
Pages 2–3. Bayside Trail, Portland, Maine. *Jerry and Marcy Monkman/EcoPhotography.*
Pages 4–5. MA'O Organic Farms, Wai'anae, Hawai'i. *Arna Johnson Photography.*
Page 6. Lake Eola Park, Orlando, Florida. *Darcy Kiefel.*
Page 8. Stonehouse Pond, Barrington, New Hampshire. *Jerry and Marcy Monkman/EcoPhotography.*
Facing page. Maywood Riverfront Park, Maywood, California. *Rich Reid Photography.*
Page 12. Three generations, KOK Ranch, Salida, Colorado. *Darcy Kiefel.*

Book design by Glyph Publishing Arts, based on concepts by Shirley Chambers
Writing and book development services by Parlandau Communications

ISBN: 978-1-932807-10-3

♻ Printed in the United States of America on 80-lb. Sterling Dull Book Recycled, which is certified by the Forest Stewardship Council (FSC), Sustainable Forestry Initiative (SFI), and Programme for the Endorsement of Forest Certification (PEFC), and contains a minimum of 10 percent post-consumer waste.

First edition 2012
10 9 8 7 6 5 4 3 2 1

To the family and friends of The Trust for Public Land,
without whom our work—and this book—would not exist.

Contents

"You cannot save the land apart from the people or the people apart from the land."

—Wendell Berry

"The experience of the past year has proven that trusted human relationships are the basic requirement for successfully acquiring and saving land."

—The Trust for Public Land's first annual report

"Our job should be to defend the true meaning of 'the public' in American life. The public good is a value we enact in all aspects of our lives, powerfully embodied in the lands we cherish and share together."

—William Cronon

"Weeds in a city lot convey the same lessons as redwoods."

—Aldo Leopold

Protecting Everyday Places

by Timothy Egan

Courtesy of Timothy Egan

THAT A TREE CAN GROW IN BROOKLYN has long been considered something of a miracle, if not a metaphor for hope. So it is in the jangle, confusion, and economic doubt of the early 21st century that we look to trees in every inner city in America—as well as in Walden Woods—to find a respite for our days and a new way to connect to the natural world.

The simple, the ordinary, the taken-for-granted are no longer such. We are an urban nation of 313 million and counting, many eyes on many pixels. "Nature's nation," as Thomas Jefferson envisioned the United States, has drifted from its link to the land, and not just because most Americans no longer get dirt under their fingernails while making their living.

So among the maladies of our age is "nature-deficit disorder"—a term coined by author Richard Louv to explain a growing disconnect between people, particularly the young, and the outdoors. He argues that obesity, depression, and a general feeling that something is missing in life can be tied to a lack of routine contact with nature. And though such a condition is not recognized by the psychology manual, I suspect that it is recognized by many people who understand *what* is missing in modern life.

And that's why The Trust for Public Land seems so suited to the great challenge of finding a balance in contemporary living by preserving—besides wilderness and national parks—lands that have a human story attached to them, lands that are not seen as distant or off-limits for all but the hardy few.

You know these places. You pass by them, perhaps daily, and don't even give them a second glance. It could be a back lot, formerly scorned as vacant, now alive as a neighborhood garden. It could be a house, once in decay and thought to be outmoded, now given its proper due as the birthplace of a heroic citizen. Or it could be a farm or ranch, a place where food or fiber has been produced

for a century, saved through a conservation easement even as it is surrounded by the creeping vines of sprawl. These are places that are vital to any society that values its open space and its past.

Yes, our national parks—"America's best idea"—offer aeries and grand vistas where a person can feel far removed from those rivers of concrete and forests of steel and glass that are habitat for most of us. More than a century ago, John Muir saw wilderness as a tonic for a frenzied era, an oasis for "thousands of tired, nerve-shaken, over-civilized people." What's more, he said that wild land was not just a luxury that a newly industrialized nation could afford but a "necessity."

When I was growing up in the West, my family never had a summer home. But we had that public land legacy—parks and national forests—mountains that looked like real-time paintings and alpine-born streams of incorrigible wildness. Because of this, my mother always said we were rich. Only later did I understand that this wealth, owned by all Americans, was a hard-earned product of Muir's tenacity with his pen and Teddy Roosevelt's force of will from the bully pulpit of the White House. Spend a year living in Europe, as I did, and you'll never doubt why American public lands are so special and make our country unique. They are crucial to our sense of self as a democracy—the shared endowment, very Jeffersonian.

But while the philosophy behind the establishment of America's protected lands has now been adopted by many countries, a new era calls for building on that with a hybrid of sorts. The singular, eye-popping settings—from the Grand Canyon to the Olympic rainforest—are protected, hopefully for the long haul. But what about the everyday places?

If people won't come to nature—as indicated by declining visits to some national parks—we need nature to come to them. Working lands and well-used urban and suburban parks shouldn't necessarily be seen as spoiled lands; they can have value without being sterile.

Not long ago I was finishing a workday in a faceless, charmless hotel in San Francisco. It didn't matter that the walls of my small room looked no different from the walls of any other enclosed space in any other city; my eyes were glued to a screen. A few hours before dusk I felt a tug of the body clock—I had to get out! A friend suggested a hike in the dun-colored hills above the sea: the Golden Gate National Recreation Area. Within minutes, without even getting into a car, I was transported to another world. It was wonderful, strolling those headlands overlooking the Pacific at that magic hour, only a few miles removed from the seven million or so people of the San Francisco metro area. I was able to lose myself.

I know now, but didn't at the time of my late-afternoon hike, that this wondrous place was a forerunner project and template for The Trust for Public Land's novel effort to protect and support land for people. Walden Woods is another of the trust's projects. But so is the schoolhouse in Topeka, Kansas, that inspired one of the great leveling decisions of the Supreme Court—*Brown v. Board of Education*, which knocked out institutionalized racial discrimination by school boards. There's nature in Newark (much more than those marshes where bodies were dumped in *The Sopranos*) and the South Bronx.

In my hometown, Seattle, what was once a badly scarred industrial site has been transformed, with considerable help from the trust, into the nine-acre Olympic Sculpture Park. This outdoor art museum, dotted with trees and native wildflowers, is on a rise looking out across Puget Sound to the Olympic Mountains. (The sunsets from here are some of the best in the world.) In a short time, the sculpture park has become one of Seattle's favorite places. It has both a story born in its gritty past—when the city was all about its brawny enterprises along the port—and a story about the future, where nature and art come together in an urban, public venue.

After 40 years, The Trust for Public Land has been instrumental in putting together more than 4,250 parks, conservation projects, and protected historic sites. They do not insist on a my-way-or-the-highway approach but rather work with agencies, private and public, who share the vision of a country connected to its history and its land.

The Columbia River Gorge may be my favorite. This is where the desert, east side of the Cascade Mountains meets up with the wet, heavily forested west side. The volcanoes of Mount Hood, Mount Adams, and Mount St. Helens, snow-topped in nearly all seasons, can be seen from bone-dry scablands along the river. The rocks are a canvas for Indian petroglyphs and a few markings from the Lewis and Clark Expedition. The wind is a constant. There are waterfalls thundering out of mountain flanks and wilderness areas in the foothills but also wineries, with grapes that grow well above the river, and many small farms. I'm told by European friends that the gorge reminds them of the best sections of the Rhine or the Danube.

But it would look and feel entirely different had not the trust taken a lead role in setting up what became the Columbia River National Scenic Area, nearly 300,000 acres of the best kind of land for people.

The earth is a product of geologic and cosmic forces far beyond our reach. But most everything attached to it comes from human hands. "We shape our buildings," said Winston Churchill, "and thereafter, our buildings shape us." He could have been talking as well about our shared spaces, small and large. Luckily for us, these places have had a guardian in The Trust for Public Land for 40 years now. It's an auspicious start.

"The Trust for Public Land does not insist on a my-way-or-the-highway approach but rather works with agencies, private and public, who share the vision of a country connected to its history and its land."

Looking Forward

by Will Rogers, President, The Trust for Public Land

Jane Bernard

THE STAFF AND VOLUNTEER LEADERSHIP of The Trust for Public Land don't spend much time looking back: we keep our eyes on the trail ahead. That focus has enabled us to adapt our conservation tools to the ever-changing challenges and opportunities presented by our mission over the past 40 years. And I'm convinced that over the next 40 years we'll continue to find new ways of working with communities to help them protect the places they care about, create healthy human habitat, and shape 21st-century cities that are not simply livable but lovable.

Our past has prepared us for the future, and it would be shortsighted to let our 40th anniversary slip by unrecognized. We are proud of what we have accomplished over the last four decades: more than 4,000 special places and 3 million acres protected; many hundreds of city parks, playgrounds, and gardens created or refurbished; and more than $33 billion in public funding raised for conservation. Even more important—but harder to quantify—are the millions of lives that have been touched by our work. Places have the power to change lives, whether it's a park or playground in a city neighborhood, the last farm in a suburban town, a much-loved beach or riverfront, or a working ranch or forest in a rural community.

The most important reason to look back on these events and accomplishments is so that we can share them with you, our supporters and friends, old and new. To you we offer this book as a reminder of (or introduction to) what we have done in the past, how it has equipped us for what are doing today, and what we must do in the future to meet radically new conservation challenges.

The Trust for Public Land was founded in the early 1970s amid a ferment of change. The environmental movement was young, conservationists were focused on habitat loss and air and water pollution, and the nation's cities were staggering

from disinvestment and discontent. The organization's founders recognized that people as well as wildlife need healthy habitat and that emerging conservation tools could be employed to conserve land for people across the American landscape, especially in cities. But their real genius was to understand that more change was inevitable, and to lodge within the soul of this new organization an entrepreneurial spirit, a commitment to people and the collective process, and a dedication to exploring new ways of solving conservation problems that no one yet knew existed.

And sure enough, 40 years later we are confronted again with a new set of challenges and opportunities. Obesity, an isolated problem in the 1970s, has become an epidemic—expensive in both human lives and health-care costs—and a crucial reason to enrich communities with health-supporting parks and greenways. Reversing the urban abandonment of the 1970s, Americans are returning to cities in search of social energy, community, and convenience—and cities are scrambling to build parks to serve current residents and attract new ones. Local farms and urban gardens are filling a vital role for more and more Americans who want to know where their food comes from. And climate change is causing us to understand that conservation must include carbon-rich forests, climate-resilient habitat, and parks and greenways to create greener, more energy-efficient cities.

Thankfully, new tools are at hand that will help us come to grips with these tasks. To help communities visualize conservation choices, we have wedded 21st-century computer mapping technologies to our long-established process of community engagement. We have refined our techniques for promoting local ballot measures—generating fuel for the public-private partnerships that drive most park and conservation projects these days. We have hired our own economist to make the concrete case

Mirror Lake, New Hampshire. Jerry and Marcy Monkman/EcoPhotography.

"The organization's founders recognized that people as well as wildlife need healthy habitat and that emerging conservation tools could be employed to conserve land for people across the American landscape, especially in cities."

for the quantifiable benefits of parks and conservation. We have perfected a participatory design process that has helped students and community members from New York to California plan parks and playgrounds and then see them come to life. Our Center for City Park Excellence has become a national leader in reporting on the services delivered by park systems nationwide and in sharing best-practice information about city parks. And our newly launched ParkScore™ project website is helping cities understand how their park systems can better serve their residents.

So please come with us as we pause for a moment to glance back even as we keep our attention focused on the problems of today and tomorrow. This book is a résumé of sorts, a record of accomplishment offered as evidence of fitness for future service. We hope you will join with us in applying the power of place and land-for-people conservation to enhance our physical, economic, and environmental health—to serve growing cities, secure a healthy food supply, combat obesity, promote fitness, address climate change, and prepare for yet-to-be-known conservation challenges beyond the horizon.

Forty Years of Conservation Innovation

THE YEAR WAS 1972. GASOLINE WAS 55 CENTS A GALLON. *The Godfather* was pulling in crowds at movie theaters. Singer-songwriter Don McLean had a hit with "American Pie." Two years after the first Earth Day, Americans were growing ever more concerned about the environment. And in San Francisco, a handful of lawyers and conservationists founded a new kind of conservation organization—focused on innovation, a businesslike approach to their work, and a special mission to conserve land for people, especially in and around cities.

Forty years later, The Trust for Public Land has protected more than 4,000 special places and created hundreds of parks nationwide. Because of TPL's work, Americans can:

- Tour a dramatic sculpture park on Seattle's waterfront or visit Santa Fe's new downtown park.
- Walk the street where Dr. Martin Luther King lived as a boy.
- Hike through Walden Woods, where Henry David Thoreau found inspiration.
- Harvest vegetables from dozens of community gardens in New York City.
- Walk a beach or view migrating monarch butterflies on the California Coast.
- Ski or snowshoe through healthy, productive timberlands in Maine and Minnesota.

A mother and daughter enjoy scenic Oak Creek Canyon near Sedona, Arizona, 1998—protected as part of a series of projects for Coconino National Forest. Dominic Oldershaw.

Surrenden Farm, Groton, Massachusetts, protected in 2006 by TPL, the town, and the Groton Conservation Trust. Jerry and Marcy Monkman/EcoPhotography.

♦ Gather with fellow residents to plan a new park or playground in Newark, New Jersey, and other cities.

♦ Visit the last farm in town in dozens of fast-growing New England communities.

♦ Look forward to a future when more and more people can say, "I walk on The Trust for Public Land's work."

These ways of experiencing a place vary greatly, as do the places themselves. But they all reveal convictions of The Trust for Public Land that have remained unchanged over 40 years: That contact with nature is essential for human health and wholeness. That all Americans deserve close-to-home parks, playgrounds, and natural areas. That a city park or garden measured in square feet can bestow benefits as deep and life-enhancing as a vast backcountry wilderness. That the most enduring parks and protected natural areas emerge from cooperative, community-based efforts that include government, business leaders, neighbors, and families. And that working with others to create a park or protect a much-loved local open space is in itself a profound way to build and strengthen a community.

The earliest project among the handful just mentioned was completed in 1973. The most recent opened in 2011. So what kind of organization is capable of sustaining a mission to protect land for people over four decades of intense change? Like the Reagan administration's efforts in the 1980s to choke off additions to national parks and refuges, or the real estate boom of the 1990s, or the economic freefall of the recent past? How did The Trust for Public Land reach its 40th birthday with a record of accomplishment and a web of public and private partnerships that position it to lead in conservation through the next 40 years? Seeking answers, these pages tell many stories. All of them highlight two legacies of the organization's founders: an inspiring mission to create parks and connect people to nature where they live, and an entrepreneurial, pragmatic approach to conservation. Without the first there would be no reason for The Trust for Public Land. Without the second, TPL would not have survived 40 years of change or be so well prepared to meet today's conservation challenges.

AN IDEA IS BORN

As the 1960s ended, leaders of the surging environmental movement in and around San Francisco were exploring new paths to protecting land. One was Huey Johnson, a broad-spectrum environmental leader who was also the western regional director for The Nature Conservancy—then, as now, one of the nation's most successful environmental groups. The Conservancy specialized in buying and holding biologically important wild lands. But Huey had been working on certain transactions in which land was resold instead to public agencies for protection. This led to a big-time insight: that a nonprofit organization, if it were flexible,

fast-moving, and knew its way around tax codes and real estate law, could play a vital role in acquiring land for public ownership and might support itself through the transactions.

By the summer of 1971, Huey had determined to test his ideas in a new organization. For strategic support, he turned to his friend and colleague Greg Archbald, one of the first California attorneys to focus on using real property law in land conservation. By early 1972 Greg was working to clarify the concept of the organization, draft founding documents and funding proposals, and plan how it would operate. As Robert Cahn, a founding Trust for Public Land board member, put it, "Huey was the visionary, Greg was the practical architect."

As the two men laid the groundwork for the new nonprofit and got feedback from wise friends and advisors, Huey carried on at The Nature Conservancy. One project on his plate was an epic land use battle close to home. Back in the mid-1960s, a developer from Pennsylvania had surveyed Gerbode Valley in the rugged Marin County headlands north of the Golden Gate and seen "the most beautiful location in the United States for a new community." With funding from Gulf Oil, "Marincello" was conceived on a grand scale: 50 apartment towers, hundreds of homes and townhouses,

Above: Celebrating the opening of Pine Avenue Park, Maywood, California, in 2011. Jonathan Alcorn. Left: Trust for Public Land founder Huey Johnson in the mid-1970s. TPL archives.

What kind of organization is capable of sustaining a mission to protect land for people over four decades of intense change?

Looking across Rodeo Lagoon into Gerbode Valley, Golden Gate National Recreation Area. Lawyers and conservationists who worked to protect the land from development would later help found TPL. Over 40 years, TPL has completed nearly a dozen projects to help build the recreation area. Robert Campbell.

a mall, and an upscale hotel at the peak of the headlands. Ignoring local opposition, Marin County approved the project in 1965, and construction of roads, gates, and freeway off-ramps began.

Environmentalists and hikers, who treasured the open, rolling landscape and had pushed for its permanent protection, were aghast. As the development's budget mounted, along with opposition, local attorneys filed a crucial lawsuit. In 1970 the court ruled

that Marincello was improperly zoned, effectively killing the project. Meanwhile, a splendid new national park, the Golden Gate National Recreation Area (GGNRA), was taking shape, and Huey Johnson convinced The Nature Conservancy to option the former Marincello lands for later acquisition by the park service.

While The Trust for Public Land had no role in protecting the Marincello land, the project came to loom large in the organization's

consciousness as a precursor to its founding. Besides Huey's work on the acquisition, two charter TPL board members, attorneys Doug Ferguson and Marty Rosen, had worked on the lawsuit that stopped the development. Also, protecting close-to-home parklands like the GGNRA would become a signal part of TPL's mission, much as the protection of wildlands was for The Nature Conservancy.

A NEW KIND OF ORGANIZATION

As Huey Johnson described The Trust for Public Land in an introductory brief, the organization was "a logical outgrowth of" and "complementary to" The Nature Conservancy. This assessment would be borne out in later years as the two organizations, in pursuit of their individual missions, often partnered on conservation projects. But there was a crucial difference. Huey believed that conservation work needed to be extended to urban areas.

"Nearly 80 percent of the nation's people live in metropolitan areas, yet only a small percentage of the existing public recreation lands are available to them," Huey wrote. He called this a "major flaw in the American dream." Building on the work of conservationists since John Muir and Teddy Roosevelt, the nation had set aside wilderness and remote open space where wild nature was protected and people with the means could go for recreation and inspiration. But Huey and other conservationists perceived a disconnect between environmentalism and the parallel drive toward social justice that had moved to the center of America's consciousness. Many city residents were as likely to visit a national park, or even a state park a few counties away, as they were to hit the lottery.

Bringing nature to these people where they lived was a matter of justice for Huey and the other TPL founders. More pragmatically, cities were where most voters lived. "We recognized that as cities grew, urban voters were going to determine all future environmental issues," Johnson recalled years later. Urban dwellers could not be expected to protect Mother Nature until they learned to love her. And they would form this attachment, Huey believed, only through nearby parks and open space—their closest points of access to the natural world. His recruitment pitch typically quoted his environmental hero, Aldo Leopold, who famously said that "weeds in a city lot convey the same lessons as redwoods."

As Huey and Greg talked with people from the Bay Area nonprofit, business, legal, and political communities, and others, the shape of the new organization emerged. It would be professionally staffed and efficiently run. It would invent its own techniques for land preservation but also apply those already pioneered by The Nature Conservancy—such as helping public agencies acquire land for parks, recreation, and conservation. It would be streamlined and responsive to the market, able to move quickly to protect conservation-worthy land as it became available.

And rather than relying on membership dues, it would support itself through its transactions. By offering landowners the tax advantages of selling to a nonprofit, TPL could purchase land at a charitable discount—receiving, in essence, a donation of land value that would be used to support the organization. (In later years, this

Many city dwellers were as likely to visit a national or state park as they were to hit the lottery. Bringing nature to people where they lived was a matter of justice for The Trust for Public Land's founders.

Left: Mori Point south of San Francisco. TPL project managers outbid developers at auction to add the land to the Golden Gate National Recreation Area in 2002. Michael Macor/San Francisco Chronicle/ Corbis. Below: A mural of a tree decorated TPL's first office above a row of shops in San Francisco. TPL archives.

Above: Annual report, 1974, The Trust for Public Land. *Right: TPL founding board members Yvonne Rand and Doug Ferguson.* TPL archives.

funding model would be unable to support the complicated and expensive work of conserving land and creating parks—especially in cities—and TPL came to rely more and more on charitable donations to support its work.)

The first board meeting took place in the guest room of a San Francisco hotel because no one had remembered to book a meeting room. Besides Doug and Marty and Greg, Huey's early recruits for the staff or board included attorney Putnam (Put) Livermore, publisher Alfred Heller, Pulitzer Prize–winning journalist Bob Cahn, retired entrepreneur Si Foote, conservationist Joel Kuperberg (who, like Marty Rosen, would eventually serve as president), and Bob McIntyre, a Harvard MBA who would manage TPL's financial affairs through its first quarter-century.

The founders briefly considered calling their nascent organization Project Lorax, after the hero of a Dr. Seuss book who spoke up for trees. But that possibility was soon jettisoned, and Huey credits Greg Archbald for the name that stuck. The intent was clear: a *trust* (a nonprofit that conserves something) founded to set aside *land for public* ownership and use.

In January 1973, the fledgling organization—with a staff of 12—moved into a second-story office over a watch shop near San Francisco's financial district. In the spirit of the times and TPL's

mission, a tree was painted on the building's exterior, its branches reaching the second floor. For working capital TPL had substantial gifts from the San Francisco Foundation, the Ford Foundation, the Andrew Norman Foundation, and an anonymous donor, as well as a $10 million line of credit with Bank of America.

The newborn nonprofit had a lot going for it, starting with smart people fueled by a strong mission, and a plausible set of assumptions that could produce success. TPL's founders believed that the urban public wanted and would pay for accessible parks and natural lands. That there was a gap in the delivery system for public open space that could only be filled by a lean, technically skilled private organization. That the tax laws offered opportunities that could make TPL at least partly self-supporting. That a young staff could be trained in the technical aspects of conservation real estate. That there was a ready pool of skilled volunteers among executive retirees from business. And finally, that innovation and experimentation could be built into the everyday operations of a well-run organization. (See "Four Founding Goals," page 26.)

But in January of 1973, no one knew just how the whole excellent idea would work in practice. The IRS had to be convinced that an organization that competed for land in the marketplace could be deemed nonprofit. And would public agencies welcome a nonprofit acquisition partner? "I don't think any of us had an undying faith that it was all going to be successful," remembers Doug Ferguson. "It was a long time before TPL had much of a track record, and those early board meetings weren't a whole lot of fun for people like me, who like to see results."

The results wouldn't be long in coming.

FOUR FOUNDING GOALS

Huey Johnson and other founders of The Trust for Public Land wanted to be very clear about their vision for the new organization. At the outset, they articulated four founding goals, and for the first half-dozen years, every annual report was organized around them. They were:

- ◆ to acquire and preserve open space to serve human needs
- ◆ to create a new profession of public land specialists
- ◆ to pioneer and share new techniques of land preservation and funding
- ◆ to operate as a self-sustaining conservation organization

In later decades, as the work grew more complicated and philanthropic funding became more important, the fourth goal gradually fell away. But the other three have proved remarkably durable. The first answers the question: why do the work? It is the heart of the mission as later expressed in the tagline: "Conserving Land for People." The other two are about how the work is done. They focus on entrepreneurship, training, partnership, and the development and sharing of conservation techniques and knowledge—all of which have been central to TPL's way of working.

The soundness of any mission statement is proved only over time. Each of these goals has been brought to life over and over throughout TPL's four decades of work. There is every reason to believe that they will continue to be tested and found good over the next 40 years.

GAINING MOMENTUM

Early in 1973, at his desk in the new TPL offices, Huey Johnson took a phone call from Nicolas Charney, the founder of *Psychology Today* magazine and then owner of Wilkins Ranch, a 1,300-acre swath of open land climbing from the head of tranquil Bolinas Lagoon to a ridgetop overlooking the Pacific Ocean. In the 19th century, timbers from Wilkins Ranch built the wharves in San Francisco, and animals raised there fed that growing city. A hundred years later the land seemed ideally suited for protection in the new GGNRA—so well suited that Huey had tried to buy it when he

was with The Nature Conservancy. "I need to raise $15,000. Are you still interested?" Charney wanted to know.

Johnson remembers this as a "sweaty moment for TPL." If the organization acquired the property, the goal would be to transfer it to the National Park Service—but there was no guarantee this would happen. He decided the risk was worth taking, and by lunchtime he was sitting in a restaurant with Charney, drafting an option agreement on a paper napkin. Later, attorney and board member Put Livermore guided TPL through a labyrinth of bureaucratic Park Service politics—a task he would continue to perform over the

An Outward Bound student on Thompson Island, protected in 2002 as part of the Boston Harbor National Recreation Area. Susan Lapides.

Right: U.S. Representative Phillip Burton, right, an architect of the Golden Gate National Recreation Area, with second TPL president Marty Rosen. Marion Brenner. Below: Huey Johnson runs an early staff meeting. TPL archives.

years—culminating in crucial meetings with the Department of the Interior in Washington.

One of three projects TPL completed in its first year, Wilkins Ranch highlighted the advantages The Trust for Public Land would bring to conservation real-estate work. It required speed and the assumption of risk, which a private nonprofit could bring to bear. If the National Park Service had had to wait for the wheels of government to turn, the property would have been lost.

The transaction also helped generate momentum for an important new type of federal public land resource. Historically, national parks had been located in remote areas, not within an hour's drive of millions of people. The GGNRA would be followed by big but accessible federal parks such as the Columbia River Gorge National Recreation Area, near Portland, Oregon; the Chattahoochee River National Recreation Area on the edge of Atlanta; and the Cuyahoga Valley National Park, south of Cleveland. In pursuit of its land-for-people mission, TPL would help to build all of these federal open spaces over the next 40 years, including nearly a dozen additions to the GGNRA.

BUSINESS SUITS AND HIKING BOOTS

"It was a heady experience to work with TPL in the first years," founding board member Bob Cahn recalled years later in an

informal memoir. "There was little in the way of rules. Huey was running an ad hoc shop, in which we were scrambling to discover what would work."

Early photographs of TPL's band of lawyers and financial experts show the men in sensible business dress surmounted by the beards, mustaches, sideburns, and shaggy hair of the 1970s. The organization thrived on "creative chaos," Cahn recalled. "TPL was a ferment of ideas ... and a meeting place for denizens of the environmental movement: young eco-freaks, blue-blood conservationists, urban guerillas, technicians, and bureaucrats." Huey Johnson liked to hire people who were gifted generalists, "skilled communicators with enough passion to move an idea into people's heads."

The small staff could quickly confer among themselves and take action with a very short chain of approval. The first board of directors—which included a Zen priest, a journalist, a vintner, a cattle rancher, a psychiatrist, and a Swedish environmentalist—was there to advise and consent, not to govern. An advisory council of volunteers shared valuable business experience and contacts, but it was mostly an honorary roster. Structures would accrete and styles would change, of course, as the organization grew up.

Among the first crew of staffers was Phillip Wallin, who would serve on TPL's staff for more than a decade and go on to help found the Western Rivers Conservancy. Phil was recruited by Huey while still a law student at the University of Chicago, "studying the futility of human life at Wrigley Field," as he later said wryly. His assignment was to write a training manual for

TPL staff titled *A Technology of Nonprofit Land Acquisition*. At 800 pages, it wasn't a handbook you could stick in your pocket when you went out to meet with a landowner, but it stood for many years as the only comprehensive text on the subject.

It was the first of many books, white papers, and reports TPL would publish over the decades to share its growing body of knowledge. As such, it helped meet other of the organization's founding goals: "to pioneer [and share] new techniques of land preservation" and "to create a new profession of public land specialists." (See "Spreading the Word," page 30.)

Another way Huey Johnson trained new staff was by showing them videotaped interviews with veteran project managers. Also getting trained were volunteer "land counselors"—retired business-people and community leaders who could be effective in convincing their peers to donate land or in facilitating a negotiation.

By the end of their first full year, Johnson and company had attracted new talent to the staff and board and begun to develop the partnership skills that would become crucial as the organization evolved. They had also gained powerful political allies such as U.S. Representative Phillip Burton—a force of nature and one of the chief architects of the GGNRA. It was no accident that Burton found kindred spirits at TPL. A thoroughly urban animal, "he'd never actually get out on the land and walk it," recalls his friend Marty Rosen, "but he'd fight the world to create a trail." TPL's mission to bring nature to city dwellers had struck a resonant chord.

The protection of Bee Canyon to create Los Angeles's O'Melveny Park was one of TPL's first urban projects. Sam Roberts.

SPREADING THE WORD

"In building TPL we have sought the best minds and the most experienced and dedicated people available, and we believe we have them. One major challenge ahead is to share this capability and our experience with others in communities across the nation."

—Huey Johnson,
in TPL's first annual report, 1975

Opposite: Selected issues of TPL's Land&People *magazine, which has shared conservation trends, techniques, and success stories since 1989. Below: Huey Johnson trains staff and volunteers in the 1970s.* Bill Ganslen.

When charter Trust for Public Land staffer Phillip Wallin was toiling away on the proto-training manual soberly titled *A Technology of Nonprofit Land Acquisition*, he couldn't have known that this 800-page tome would be just the first trickle in a deluge of training materials and publications issued by TPL over the next four decades. The organization's founders were clear in their intent to "professionalize" the work of land conservation—which meant training, educating, and providing tools not just for staff but also for conservation volunteers and public agency employees around the country. Stated simply, the ambitious goal was to "share knowledge of nonprofit land acquisition processes."

Early staff got up to speed by studying Wallin's manual, which summarized TPL's operating methods through case studies and narrative instruction—an approach basic to studying law or business but new to the field of resource management. They were also exposed to videotaped seminars with veteran staff, and tested their mettle in role-play exercises with "landowners." Very soon they began to spread the word, training community groups in the practical realities of securing land in the marketplace,

including, as Wallin put it, "the real estate skills traditionally used to destroy neighborhoods."

Much of this teaching took place in the course of TPL's work with land trusts, both urban and rural. In the late 1970s, workshops were offered to help local groups convert vacant city land into community parks and gardens: in Boston, Denver, and other cities. Some were sponsored by the U.S. Interior Department's Heritage Conservation and Recreation Service (HCRS), for whom TPL produced a booklet called *Citizens Action Manual: A Guide to Recycling Vacant Property*. It was widely circulated, as was a follow-up publication, *A Citizens' Guide to Maintaining Neighborhood Places*.

As land trusts increasingly became the ground troops for local conservation, TPL embarked on an expanded effort to share land acquisition skills, through its foundation-funded National Land Counselor Program. Each year for four years, it offered intensive training to land trust staff—a week of classes followed by in-the-field transaction experience with TPL project managers.

In later years, as TPL developed expertise in specialized conservation areas, it moved quickly to share what it was learning in books, reports, white papers, and eventually websites. The process was: experiment, learn, and then share what was learned. Conserving watersheds, recycling urban brownfields into parks, using conservation easements to protect ranchlands, raising state and local conservation funds through bond and tax measures, setting up comprehensive community conservation programs to spend locally raised funds, and the economic, health, and social benefits of parks and conservation: TPL has published on all these topics.

Today the knowledge goes out (usually with pictures!) through many channels in print and online: from TPL's website, online databases such as the LandVote tally of conservation finance measures, and the City Parks Blog on urban park issues. Twice a year, TPL serves up a generous feast of words and images in *Land&People* magazine. More information is available from eNews: monthly emails to supporters on the latest land conservation news near them and across the nation, and the *LandLink* and *Washington Watch* e-newsletters for conservation professionals.

Koshland Park, shown here in 1977, was San Francisco's biggest new park in more than 40 years. TPL archives.

LAND FOR CITY PEOPLE

Almost immediately after its founding, The Trust for Public Land began the work that would ripen into today's Parks for People initiative—an effort to create parks and conserve open space in American cities.

The ink was barely dry on TPL's incorporation papers when the public-spirited Los Angeles lawyer John O'Melveny tapped the organization to handle a transaction transferring his C.J. Ranch in Bee Canyon to the city's Department of Parks and Recreation. Today, 672-acre O'Melveny Park is L.A.'s fourth-largest park. Protecting Bee Canyon was TPL's first urban project; its work in the metropolis would eventually lead to dozens of new parks and protected areas in park-deprived neighborhoods, along the abused Los Angeles River, in the shadow of China-town, and, perhaps most famously, on Cahuenga Peak, the land behind the Hollywood Sign.

Around the same time, TPL was given the opportunity to build a park in its own backyard, when a leading San Francisco philanthropic family asked it to create a park in honor of its patriarch, Daniel Koshland, on the occasion of his 80th birthday. Working with the Koshland family, TPL quietly acquired two lots in the crowded, low-income neighborhood of Hayes Valley, tore down an existing structure that had recently suffered a fire, combined the lots to create a park based on neighborhood goals, and presented it to the city in Mr. Koshland's name. It was San Francisco's largest new park in more than 40 years. TPL's first inner-city park project set the tone for similar efforts in San Francisco and other cities for the next 40 years: uniting private philanthropy, neighborhood participation, and municipal support to answer a pressing community need.

The nation's cities were at a low ebb around the time of TPL's founding. "Urban renewal" projects of the 1960s had often blighted more than they renewed, and the desperate quality of life in the inner cities had fueled riots during the latter part of that decade. Americans sympathized with the plight of inner-city kids who lacked trees to climb and lakes to swim in, and plenty of summer camps and programs sprang up to whisk children away for short-term recreation and relief from the mean streets. But that wasn't a real solution: people needed access to nature where they lived. Inadequate parks and recreation programs were a common complaint in half of the cities surveyed for a 1968 report on the riots issued by the National Advisory Commission on Civil Disorders.

TPL's leaders also believed that, aside from the tangible benefits of outdoor play and refreshment parks could provide, the process of park-building itself was important. Quite a few early staffers had worked in community organizing and were predisposed to the idea that bringing residents together to protect community land could infuse a neighborhood with a much-needed sense of pride, empowerment, and ownership. This is turn could mobilize residents to work for other social goals.

> "The need for urban open space is particularly acute. Even though we have discovered that working on projects in urban centers sometimes means extensive costs, the social significance more than justifies the expense."
>
> —Annual report, 1974, The Trust for Public Land

In 1976, TPL acquired four acres to create San Francisco's Potrero del Sol Park. Bonnie Trach.

TPL only needed to look across San Francisco Bay to find a community both desperately in need of natural space and well supplied with vacant, rubble-strewn lots that might host parks or gardens. Oakland was fertile ground for an ambitious experiment in "land banking," as Huey Johnson called it. If TPL could amass enough of those lots—mostly owned by local banks by way of foreclosures—it could team with residents to begin the greening of Oakland.

So began the work that evolved into TPL's National Urban Land Program, which within a few years established beachheads in Newark, New Jersey; New York City; and Miami and

Above and below: TPL quickly expanded its urban work to Oakland, creating miniparks and gardens. TPL archives. Opposite: Clinton Community Garden, an early project after TPL expanded to New York City in 1978. Ken Sherman.

Fort Lauderdale, Florida. By 1977, TPL had established 15 land trusts in these cities and acquired 53 properties on their behalf.

TPL's Oakland Land Project did eventually acquire dozens of vacant properties—as donations from banks or for payment of back taxes—and pass them on to community groups to be transformed into miniparks, gardens, and playgrounds. Community partners included neighborhood and church groups, even (briefly) the Black Panthers. Residents collaborated on the design of the green spaces with landscape architects and students from the University of California at Berkeley, brought in by TPL. At the 39th Avenue Garden, residents hand-dug a well and erected a 39-foot windmill to pump the water.

Unfortunately, many of these parks and gardens failed to survive, and TPL learned a vital lesson about the importance of training local groups to accept ongoing stewardship. Ensuring stewardship is now a vital part of all TPL park projects. In later years, TPL carefully shepherded other park projects in Oakland: renovating the quarter-acre Bertha Port Park in West Oakland, and collaborating with the city and the Friends of Bella Vista Park to transform a bleak asphalt playground into a beautiful 1.6-acre park in Oakland's densely populated San Antonio district.

EASTWARD HO!

On a sunny June morning in 2008, Mayor Cory Booker and TPL broke ground for Newark's largest city-owned park, serving 7,000 neighborhood children. Nat Turner Park represented a high point in an ongoing and productive park effort that began in 1976 when The Trust for Public Land opened its first East Coast office in that city.

Back then, Newark was popularly seen as an archetypal urban wasteland. But the city owned more than 4,000 abandoned lots that could be put to good use, and two local foundations asked TPL to help. The challenge was to stimulate the neighborhood energy and cooperation needed to turn those derelict properties into something useful and beautiful. To tackle it, Huey sent Peter Stein, a University of California, Santa Cruz, graduate and veteran of the Oakland Land Project, and Lisa Cashdan—both of whom remain close to TPL as supporters and advisors to this day. To turn some of those vacant lots into playgrounds, Stein's tiny team convinced the local phone company to supply telephone poles for the construction of play structures. A tire company donated tires for swings, and a drug company provided barrels for making tunnels. (None of these would be acceptable as playground materials by today's stricter standards.)

TPL arrived in Newark, New Jersey, in the mid-1970s and is still creating parks there nearly 40 years later. Above: Nat Turner Park, 2009. J. Avery Wham Photography.

More than 30 years later, thanks to a well-established partnership with the city and generous foundation support, TPL continues to help bring parks and playgrounds to Newark residents. Nat Turner Park is one of ten new community parks that TPL has helped to create in Newark over the last few years.

Having set all this in motion, Stein and Cashdan carried TPL's urban work across the Hudson River in 1978, establishing the New York City Urban Land Program. The work was very similar to that in Oakland and Newark: helping community residents establish land trusts, gardens, and small parks. TPL also began working to protect the city's remaining open space. "We started to apply our real estate tools to New York's last open space frontiers, which were vacant lands in the inner city and natural areas of the waterfront," says Andy Stone, who joined TPL's New York staff in 1988 and today directs its work in the city. On its 40th birthday, TPL can claim 300 park, garden, and open space projects there, from the South Bronx to downtown Brooklyn to Manhattan's Lower East Side. They include dozens of vest-pocket parks and community gardens,

more than 150 community playgrounds and parks created from barren asphalt schoolyards, and important protected natural areas along the city's harbor and rivers.

PUBLIC LANDS FOR PUBLIC ENJOYMENT

It's a long way from the gritty streets of Newark or New York to the pristine whitewater rivers of Idaho, where Trust for Public Land project manager Tom Macy found himself in 1975. Macy, a charter staff member, Vietnam vet, and devoted fly-fisherman, came north to work with federal land managers and wary locals to protect lands along the state's Wild and Scenic Rivers. Those lands in the superb high country of the Sawtooth Valley overlapped with the newly designated Sawtooth National Recreation Area. These were TPL's first projects for the Forest Service—an effort that by 2012 would reach more than 760 projects protecting nearly 580,000 acres.

In the words of an early TPL annual report, the goal of the Public Lands Program was "to acquire key parcels of open space in ways that benefit landowners, land-buying agencies, and the public." As public land managers started to become aware of TPL's capabilities—in part through attending its workshops on land acquisition—the work that began with helping to build the Golden Gate National Recreation Area expanded to Idaho, Florida, Nevada, New Jersey, Ohio, and other states.

Some project locations were remote, such as the Sawtooths. But just as often projects aimed to protect natural and recreation lands within easy reach of U.S. cities. For example, in 1978, TPL completed the first of a long series of projects to help create the Cuyahoga Valley National Recreation Area, now a 33,000-acre national park and one of the nation's premier close-to-home natural and historic areas. Only a short drive from both Cleveland and Akron, the park epitomizes TPL's goal of allowing millions of residents each year to find natural beauty and recreational opportunities not far from their doorstep. By 2012, TPL had completed more than 20 projects there, most recently protecting the Cleveland Orchestra's Blossom Music Center in the heart of the park.

To handle the growing volume of public lands transactions, TPL needed troops on the ground. The founding goal of "creating a new profession of public interest land specialists" became a necessity. TPL project managers were—and are—transaction facilitators. Their role was to learn the needs of the landowner and the public agency that might assume eventual ownership, work out where funding would come from and how the land would be managed, and get buy-in from local groups and officials whose support could be critical. Project managers were lawyers, planners, business school graduates, or corporate refugees, who might wear hiking boots on weekends but showed up at meetings in wingtips or pumps, ready to talk business.

In 1978, TPL completed the first of a long series of projects to help create what is now the Cuyahoga Valley National Park. Tom Jones.

"As a project manager I discovered the excitement of knowing there's some great piece of land or a new park that wouldn't be there except for my personal efforts—negotiating, working late nights, sweating blood to make it happen."

—Ernest Cook,
TPL senior vice president

Right: Jennie Gerard, director of the 1980s Land Trust Program. TPL archives. Below: Members of the Taos Land Trust, one of hundreds of local land trusts established with TPL's help. Ingrid Lundahl.

Beyond business skills, they required adaptability, resourcefulness, and commitment to a community's needs.

The nature of the work kept TPL entrepreneurial and tightly focused on the achievable. In the early years, budgets were so small that a single project might generate 25 to 30 percent of TPL's support for a year. If a project fell through at the last minute—and more than a few did—not only might the land be lost, but weeks of work could go unreimbursed, endangering the organization and its mission. For this reason, project work seemed to attract the kind of people who measured themselves by their ability to perform when the stakes were high. The work was exciting, and the product was tangible. You could "walk on your work," as project managers grew fond of saying. Often TPL was asked to take on the toughest and most complicated transactions, giving rise to another favorite phrase around the shop: "If someone else could do it, we wouldn't be there."

THE KITCHEN BRIGADES

In 1977, Huey Johnson announced that he was resigning from The Trust for Public Land to become California's secretary of resources in the first Jerry Brown administration. For its second president, TPL turned to Joel Kuperberg, who had opened TPL's Southeast Regional office in Tallahassee, Florida, a few years

earlier. Joel had caught Huey's attention with his leadership of the Collier County Conservancy, a local land trust, and once he was president, Joel expanded TPL's work in this realm. Soon the Land Trust Program joined the Urban Land Program and the Public Land Program as the tripartite focus of TPL's work. To head up the program, Joel hired Jennie Gerard, a planning professional with experience in training and workshops.

Land trusts are nonprofits that work locally or across a region or state to protect land. A land trust may acquire and hold land through purchase or donation, or may protect it by buying or accepting donation of a conservation easement—a legal agreement that guides how the land will be used by its current owner and subsequent owners. Easements are often used to prevent or limit development.

As of 2010, there were more than 1,700 land trusts nationwide, and land protected by them totaled more than 47 million acres. But when TPL was founded, only a handful of land trusts existed outside New England. In February 1978, the organization sponsored the first land trust conference in the West in its San Francisco offices. Most of TPL's work with land trusts was in the field, however. "Kitchen brigades" under Jennie's direction carried the message to wherever local groups hoped to protect open space and community character.

"I spent a lot of time in Colorado and Wyoming," Jennie recalled years later. "All over California, all over the Northwest." She and fellow staffers sounded out groups in advance, then often hit three

or four on each trip—meeting with members on nights and weekends, staying in their homes, sleeping on their couches. They taught workshops on the legal aspects of trusts; on fundraising, organizing, and using conservation easements. "It was wonderful to be with these groups of people who were discovering their potential, excited about what they might do and excited about showing you the land they loved," she recalled. "It was an incredible high."

Over the 1980s and '90s, TPL helped to found or train about a third of the nation's land trusts—then totaling about 1,200—in communities from Jackson Hole, Wyoming, to Kaua'i in Hawai'i; Taos, New Mexico; and the Thousand Islands in upstate New York. In terms of TPL's own growth, noted Bob Cahn, "land trusts could be … a constituency of true believers, our eyes and ears in communities throughout the nation."

As the movement spread in the West, a distinct focus emerged: using land trusts to protect agricultural and other "working"

lands such as ranches or productive forests. In the late 1970s, TPL was a prominent advisor to the founders of Marin Agricultural Land Trust, which to date has protected more than 25,500 acres north of San Francisco. TPL went on to help form land trusts to benefit orchardists in Colorado, dairy farmers in Washington State, and cattle ranchers in Wyoming. Later, ranchers prominent in TPL-created land trusts helped found a national group, the American Farmland Trust.

As land trusts proliferated in the early 1980s—especially after the expansion of federal tax benefits for conservation easements—TPL helped launch the Land Trust Alliance, a national group that would assume responsibility for convening and training such groups. "TPL was the Johnny Appleseed of the land trust movement in the 1970s and '80s," says Rand Wentworth, who ran TPL's Atlanta field office for many years and is now president of the Alliance. "The trust did more than anyone to bring the movement national."

> "TPL was the Johnny Appleseed of the land trust movement in the 1970s and '80s. The trust did more than anyone to bring the movement national."
>
> —Rand Wentworth, president, Land Trust Alliance

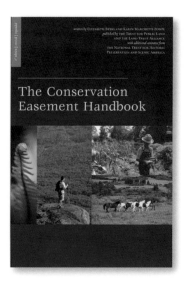

The Conservation
Easement Handbook

Today TPL and the Alliance work hand in hand to promote conservation funding and legislation. TPL frequently partners with local land trusts that need its legal, financial, or transaction expertise to complete a project.

HARD TIMES FOR PUBLIC LANDS

In 1979, Joel Kuperberg left the Trust for Public Land presidency to work on special projects and plant TPL's flag in the Northwest. Taking his place as president was Martin J. Rosen, a transportation lawyer, veteran of Marin County conservation battles, and founding TPL board member. Marty, who agreed to take the position "temporarily," ultimately served for nearly 20 years and oversaw dramatic organizational growth. By the time he left in 1998, TPL had 240 staff members working from 25 offices and was closing in on its millionth acre of conserved land.

That record almost didn't happen. Not long after Marty became president of TPL, Ronald Reagan became president of the United States and appointed as his secretary of the interior James G. Watt, who promptly announced a moratorium on federal land

acquisitions. Appropriations from the federal Land and Water Conservation Fund—the primary source of funds for the agencies that bought TPL's land—quickly plummeted to a fraction of what they had been during the Carter administration. Key TPL projects simply stalled.

For example, at the Golden Gate National Recreation Area, the moratorium delayed acquisition of Sweeney Ridge—the hilltop south of San Francisco from which Spanish explorer Gaspar de Portola spotted San Francisco Bay in 1769. Ralph Benson, then TPL's general counsel and later its chief operating officer, remembers how the local congressional delegation worked to get the land into the recreation area even as the park system resisted.

One day Ralph and TPL's federal affairs manager Harriet Burgess were summoned by U.S. Representative Phil Burton to the office of Jack Davis, the park service's acting regional director. Also present were local U.S. representatives Tom Lantos and Pete McCloskey. On Burton's instructions, Davis dialed park service director Russ Dickenson in D.C. "The three congressmen proceeded to shout into the little box that was then speaker-phone technology, all

Above: Published by TPL and the Land Trust Alliance, The Conservation Easement Handbook *is a bible for local land trusts nationwide. Right: A 50,000-acre Everglades project had to be reconfigured after federal funding faltered in the early 1980s.* Buddy Mays/Corbis.

telling Dickenson to act on our appraisal," Ralph recalls. But in the end, Sweeney Ridge was not transferred to the National Park Service until after Watt's resignation in 1984.

The delay that most threatened TPL's future arose in connection with a public land acquisition near Everglades National Park in Florida—TPL's largest project to date. Based on an understanding that the National Park Service would repurchase the land, TPL had invested considerable time and money to acquire 49,800 acres from the Aerojet Missile subsidiary of Ohio-based General Tire, which had scuttled plans to build a major facility there. Preserving this huge parcel would go a long way toward helping address water quality issues in the park. But now the project stalled, and if it sank, it might take TPL down with it. Fortunately—thanks in part to Joel Kuperberg's deep connections in Florida—the land was bought instead by the South Florida Water Management District and the State of Florida for a state park, protecting its wetlands and the water quality of the Everglades.

NEW DIRECTIONS

Despite a hostile administration, the conservation community fairly quickly worked out a way to finance important federal projects: by working directly with legislators to fund specific projects out of the Land and Water Conservation Fund (LWCF). Under the federal affairs leadership of Harriet Burgess, TPL was a key player along with The Wilderness Society in developing what became known as the "conservationists' alternative budget"—an annual list of deliverable projects that were already under contract and ready for conservation. "The legislative branch would fund them and the executive branch would have to buy them even if they didn't want to," says Ralph Benson. "The system continued into the early 1990s, and I believe the LWCF might well have withered away and died but for the conservationists' alternative budget." To this day, TPL's federal affairs group maintains an active role working with legislators and promoting the LWCF, not only for TPL's own projects but for the entire conservation community.

Nevertheless, the playing field had changed for conservation, imperiling the Public Lands Program and even TPL's ability to pursue its broader mission. "There were more than a few occasions when it seemed like it might be time to count the lifeboats," founding board member Doug Ferguson remembered years later. He recalled a board meeting around the time when Watt's moratorium was beginning to bite: "We looked at the numbers, and I said, as a businessperson I think our business model is shot. If

you're selling buggy whips and you look out the window and see cars running by, you do one of two things: you either close your doors or you start making cars." The essence of Marty Rosen's response, as Doug recalls, was "Okay, we're going to make cars."

What his friend meant, says Doug, was "Let's redefine our business. If we can't work with the feds at this point, we'll do business with states and local governments." At this moment, Rosen's belief that you can find solutions if you just look hard enough set the tone for organizational shifts that followed. He says, "If you're deeply engaged with what you're doing, thoughtful, competent, then you have to have a measure of confidence that you will find a way out of the canyon."

"An injunction went out to every staff member that the first and foremost job was to start thinking about alternatives," Doug recalls. "That turned TPL in a new direction, leaving the federal door open but creating a whole new set of options we're exploring to this day."

As the responsibility for protecting land fell more heavily on states, counties, and municipalities, it made sense to develop those relationships. TPL began helping those governments inventory lands, assess the needs and preferences of neighborhoods, and

Sweeney Ridge, an addition to the Golden Gate National Recreation Area, was finally conveyed to the National Park Service in 1984, as federal funding began to recover. Michael K. Nichols.

"There were more than a few occasions when it seemed like it might be time to count the lifeboats."

—Doug Ferguson, founding board member

WATERSHED ACHIEVEMENTS

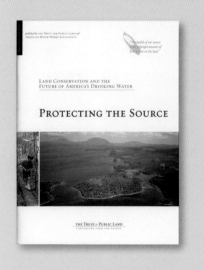

Sterling Forest, on the New York–New Jersey border is more than just a pretty woodland. The 17,500-acre forest gathers drinking water for more than a quarter of New Jersey's population. In the mid-1990s the forest's private owners proposed the construction of 13,000 homes, 8 million square feet of commercial and industrial development, and three golf courses. New Jersey officials calculated that this would so pollute the watershed that a new filtration plant would be required. Estimated cost: $160 million. Instead the state offered to contribute a mere $10 million to an effort by The Trust for Public Land and the Open Space Institute to conserve the land.

Beginning in the 1990s, as development pushed farther into remote landscapes, communities and government agencies concluded that it was cheaper to conserve watersheds than to clean up polluted water. Through its publications and in partnership with water companies and the U.S. Environmental Protection Agency (EPA), TPL has played a leading role in promoting watershed conservation and helping communities nationwide conserve land to preserve clean water.

Right: Government Canyon, Texas. Eric Swanson. *Below: Mountain Island Lake, North Carolina.* Ken Sherman. *Opposite: Sterling Forest, New York.* George M. Aronson.

In 1997, TPL published *Protecting the Source,* a report highlighting the case for protecting watersheds and describing successful watershed conservation projects. With more than 15,000 copies distributed to communities nationwide, the report proved so successful that it was expanded and republished in 2004 in partnership with the American Waterworks Association. A companion volume, *The Source Protection Handbook,* is intended—as the name implies—to take communities through the steps of watershed conservation. In 2005, TPL teamed with the U.S. EPA to publish the results of five demonstration projects to protect source water around the country, in *Path to Protection.*

Even as TPL was talking the talk, it was also walking the walk in watershed conservation projects nationwide. In North Carolina, TPL partnered with Mecklenburg County and local communities to conserve land along the shoreline and feeder streams of Mountain Island Lake—source of drinking water for more than a half million people around Charlotte—completing more than a dozen projects over a decade. In south-central Texas, TPL partnered with communities, conservation groups, and government agencies to conserve land over sensitive sections of the Edwards Aquifer, water source for more than 2 million users around Austin and San Antonio. TPL's many other watershed conservation programs include efforts around Barnegat Bay, New Jersey; in northern Ohio; and along Georgia's Chattahoochee River, source of water for 3.5 million people, including 70 percent of residents in metro Atlanta.

Forty Years of Conservation Innovation   43

As the 1980s spilled into the '90s, the drive to innovate and diversify meant new kinds of lands to save, as well as new ways of going about it.

devise bond initiatives and other funding strategies. Often TPL could generate support for a local conservation bond measure by optioning prime parcels that would otherwise be lost. Such efforts laid tracks for the more broad-based, sophisticated public finance efforts TPL developed in the 1990s. (See "Follow the Money," page 54.) And by working with local land trusts, which rely chiefly on private support, TPL could align its market-based approach to preservation with growing popular sentiment that the private sector should play a larger role in funding good public works.

"Thinking about alternatives" led in many directions. To help cash-strapped communities acquire valuable lands, TPL obtained loans from foundations and insurance companies at below-market interest rates to finance installment sales and lease-purchase options. TPL grew more sophisticated at combining and splitting parcels, and assembling funds from different sources. Sometimes land was purchased using mitigation funds—money paid under legal judgments against polluters or in the wake of environmental accidents, or by developers to compensate for habitat losses elsewhere.

Right: A Civil War reenactor at the Chickamauga and Chattanooga National Military Park, which TPL has helped to build in a series of projects. John Rawlston. Below: A TPL loan helped create Blue Hole Regional Park in Wimberley, Texas.

LAND FOR ALL REASONS

As the 1980s spilled into the '90s, The Trust for Public Land's drive to innovate and diversify meant exploring new kinds of lands to save, as well as new ways of going about it. In several cities TPL began long-term efforts to create linear parks and greenways, projects that could be immensely complicated to accomplish. A classic example is the Gwynns Falls Trail, a 14-mile hiking and biking trail through the city of Baltimore that took a decade and a half of effort on the part of TPL and its partners to complete. The trail follows the Gwynns Falls stream valley from Leakin Park near historic Franklintown, through 2,000 acres of parkland, more than 30 neighborhoods, and numerous historic and cultural sites before arriving at Baltimore's Inner Harbor.

"We've seen in city after city how greenways can connect neighborhoods, provide for recreation, and encourage renewal," TPL's Mid-Atlantic Regional Director Rose Harvey told *Land & People* magazine in 2005. TPL worked to build other greenways in the 1990s: on Atlanta's Chattahoochee River; the Los Angeles River; the Miami River; the Woonasquetucket River in Providence, Rhode Island; Boston's Neponset River; and the St. Croix River near the Twin Cities in Minnesota. With TPL's support, Chattanooga has become the poster child for the transformative effects of waterfront greenways, helping to make that city the envy of the South for its thriving economy based on quality of life and easy access to open space.

TPL also focused on watershed projects, as communities came to recognize that often the cheapest way to prevent pollution of water sources was to conserve land along streams, rivers, lakes, and reservoirs—a fact highlighted in TPL's 1997 report *Protecting the Source*. One important watershed protection effort was launched in the 425,000-acre Barnegat Bay watershed on New Jersey's coast—an effort that continues to this day. In the New York–New Jersey Highlands, TPL helped conserve 17,500-acre Sterling Forest, a source of water for a quarter of New Jersey's residents. And in Texas, long-term TPL efforts launched in the 1990s have helped protect the water quality of the Edwards Aquifer, the drinking water source for Austin, San Antonio, and other cities. TPL's work in Austin also helped maintain the cleanliness of Barton Springs, that city's iconic natural swimming hole downtown. (See "Watershed Achievements," page 42.)

Another emerging category of projects formed around preserving places important to America's history and identity—an effort that was later formalized as TPL's Heritage Lands initiative. This effort had begun a decade earlier, after some members of Congress approached TPL for help with creating a new national

Enjoying Spring Garden Point Park on the Miami River in Miami. TPL helped acquire land for the park as part of its efforts to create a greenway along the river. Darcy Kiefel.

TPL soon came to understand that its heritage work was a crucial part of its mission to protect land for all Americans.

historic site in the boyhood neighborhood of Dr. Martin Luther King. Working quickly, TPL purchased several rundown homes that had been scheduled for imminent demolition; they became the heart of the Martin Luther King Jr. National Historic Site, which today receives more than a million visitors each year.

Iconic heritage protections that followed in the 1980s and 1990s included the Melrose mansion in Natchez, Mississippi, deemed the finest Greek Revival mansion in the South; the Connecticut homestead of famed impressionist painter J. Alden Weir; the Potomac River viewshed from George Washington's home at Mount Vernon; the schoolhouse in Topeka, Kansas, that was at the center of the *Brown v. Board of Education* civil rights decision; and additions to the Franklin D. Roosevelt National Historic Site in Hyde Park, New York, and Henry David Thoreau's Walden Woods.

TPL soon came to understand that this work was a crucial part of its mission to protect land for all Americans. (See "Land for All Americans," page 48.) In 1996, a special type of TPL's Heritage Lands work reached critical mass with the founding of

the Tribal & Native Lands Program to protect land for Native Americans—peoples with land-based cultures who had been deprived of most of their lands. Over the next decade, TPL worked with more than 70 tribes to protect more than 200,000 acres for ownership or control.

Native lands projects and projects like the Martin Luther King historic site or the Monroe School confirm that conservation can serve the cause of social justice, says Marty Rosen. "It's not an accident we worked diligently to create the MLK historic district," he says. "I'm not sure Muir or Thoreau would have called that a conservation project—but we are seeking to broaden conservation to include other ethical values. These efforts in turn will contribute to the agenda of conserving land for people."

LAND FOR GREENER CITIES

In the mid-1990s, The Trust for Public Land injected new energy into its city work with the launch of the Green Cities Initiative. The program aimed to create and rehabilitate city park systems by recruiting community support, providing planning help to local governments, and developing new sources of public funding. In part, it was a response to renewed waves of inner-city unrest in the early 1990s, including six days of rioting in Los Angeles after a jury acquitted four police officers of the videotaped beating of black motorist Rodney King. Rising gang activity there and in other cities sparked urgent concern for the children drawn so early into criminal pursuits. But even in the parts of L.A. ravaged by rioting, community gardens and parks had been spared. And a manifesto issue by gang leaders listed a shortage of neighborhood parks and green spaces as among their prime complaints.

With support from the Lila Wallace–Reader's Digest Fund, TPL studied park and recreation needs and opportunities in 35 major cities. The results of this and other research were gathered in a 1994 publication called *Healing America's Cities*—a clarion call for the nation to reinvest in urban parks, recreation facilities, and open space. The report offered evidence that urban recreation holds down crime and delinquency while building self-esteem among inner-city youth. Sharpe James, then mayor of Newark, famously said, "We are going to recreate or we are going to incarcerate."

In pursuit of solutions, TPL ramped up its park-creation efforts in a dozen cities nationwide, expanding that number to 30 cities

TPL project manager Dave Vasarhelyi walks with his daughters at Canal Basin Park in Cleveland, a focus city for TPL's 1990s Green Cities Initiative. Darcy Kiefel.

LAND FOR ALL AMERICANS

"TPL protects land *for* communities, not *from* communities. Our mission differentiates TPL from other conservation organizations."

—Bowen Blair, former TPL senior vice president

Along the Columbia River in Washington, members of the Yakama Indian nation fish for salmon at a historic tribal fishing site that almost became a subdivision. In the high country above Santa Fe, Hispanic pilgrims flock to the Santuario de Chimayo, set in a pastoral tapestry of conserved farmlands. On Boston's Beacon Hill, the expanded African Meeting House, a nexus for abolitionism in the 19th century, has become a major stop on the Black Heritage Trail. And in the East Colfax neighborhood of Denver, newly arrived immigrants from Somalia and other war-torn countries plant the foods of their homelands in a spacious community garden.

Because The Trust for Public Land protects land explicitly for human use, it serves as great a diversity of Americans as any national conservation organization. Partly this is because TPL works in such a wide range of places and on so many different kinds of projects, from conserving wilderness and ranchland to creating suburban and city parks. America is a rainbow nation, and TPL works in every corner of it with people of every color.

Sometimes TPL has set out deliberately to protect lands of significance to certain populations. The most obvious example is the Tribal & Native Lands Program, which seeks to help protect land for Native Americans—historically land-based peoples who have been largely deprived of their traditional lands. Bowen Blair,

Above: A Somali immigrant gardener in Denver. Darcy Kiefel. *Top: Pipe Springs National Monument, Minnesota.* National Park Service. *Right: Santuario de Chimayo, New Mexico.* Don J. Usner.

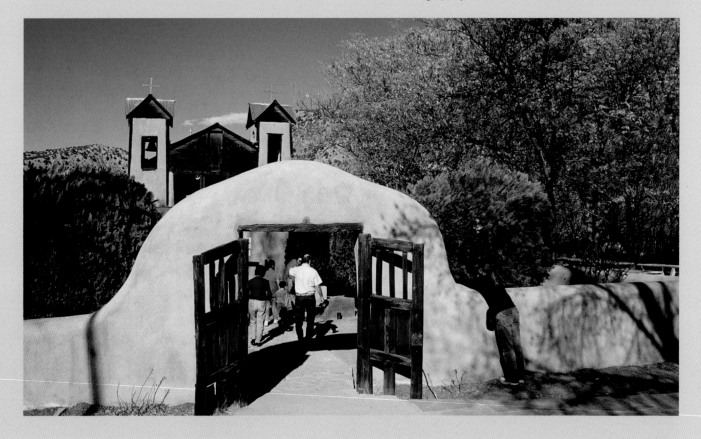

a former TPL vice president who founded the program, saw it as a "natural extension" of TPL's land-for-people mission. "TPL protects land *for* communities, not *from* communities," Bowen wrote in 2009. "Our mission differentiates TPL from other conservation organizations and resonates with tribes and Native peoples."

Although TPL had been working with Native Americans since 1989, the program was formalized in 1996 on the completion of a landmark effort to protect 10,000 acres in the Wallowa Mountains of northeast Oregon for ownership by the Nez Perce Tribe. This land was the heart of the Nez Perce historic homeland before they were forced off it by the U.S. Army at the beginning of the Nez Perce War in 1877. (See "Chief Joseph Ranch," page 136.)

Through this experience, Bowen and other TPL staffers realized that TPL's services were needed throughout Indian country. They assembled an advisory board of Native American leaders and conservationists, hired a Native American executive director, and soon were working with tribes and native groups nationwide. In Washington State, TPL helped the Quinault Tribe resolve a 130-year-old land dispute and recover 15,000 acres left out of their reservation when it was enlarged in 1873. On Cape Cod, the program helped the Mashpee Wampanaog protect a historic burial ground with a conservation easement. And in the Hawaiian islands, TPL conserved for ownership by the state's Office of Hawaiian Affairs the 25,000-acre Wao Kele o Puna rainforest on the Big Island, where generations of Native Hawaiians have hunted and foraged. To date, TPL's Tribal & Native Lands Program has helped 70 tribes and native groups protect 200,000 acres.

Members of the Northwest Band of the Shoshone Nation celebrate the return of the Bear River Massacre site in Idaho, where an estimated 350 tribal members were killed in 1863. TPL acquired the land for the tribe in 2003. Phil Schermeister.

manage it successfully. TPL's state-of-the-art services for working with communities, engaging them in park planning and design, and training them in stewardship, were acquired on the ground over years of trial and error. As Green Cities director Kathy Blaha said, "The idea is to engage people enough from the start so that they'll want to manage it later."

That was certainly the case when TPL launched its New York City Playgrounds program in 1996. Some of the first playgrounds were built on unused open space that TPL secured from the city. More recently, TPL has worked with partners to convert barren asphalt schoolyards to real community parks. "We discovered that we needed to find schools with active after-school programs run by community-based groups," says TPL's Andy Stone. "Those groups based at schools were natural partners. Having a community-oriented principal at the school was important too." TPL also promoted community engagement through a participatory design process that involved students in planning playgrounds. (See "Landscape Architecture 101," page 51.) In 2011, TPL celebrated the completion of its 50th playground in New York City—the most recent ones developed in partnership with Mayor Michael Bloomberg's PlaNYC environmental initiative. (In addition to rebuilding more than 50 playgrounds from start to finish, TPL has helped plan and rebuild more than 100 others.)

Green Cities helped TPL mature in important ways, says Vice President Ernest Cook, who helped guide the program. Before this time, TPL pursued much of its work project by project, based largely on whether staff thought an effort could be completed successfully. But the Wallace Foundation wanted a more strategic approach. "We had a great opportunity, but they said, you're not ready for it. You need to come up with a plan and define the part the foundation should support." To do this, "the regional directors had to make a commitment to do work in certain cities over a period of years: decide on the places and goals, plan how it would be funded," Cook says. The process helped move TPL to a more strategic approach in later years.

Top: In Portland, Oregon, a focus city for the initiative, TPL helped acquire Whitaker Pond in 1997. Scott Rolfson. *Above: Published as part of TPL's Green Cities Initiative, the* Healing America's Cities *report made the case for urban parks.*

in 1997. New field offices were opened in Baltimore, New Haven, Atlanta, Miami, Austin, Denver, Los Angeles, and Chattanooga. By 1998, Green Cities director Kathy Blaha could report that TPL had completed 334 park projects and helped to raise $4 billion in new state and local public funding for parks.

TPL was learning that urban projects could be exceedingly challenging, says Marty Rosen. "They're much more difficult than doing a single transaction with the Forest Service. You're dealing with many different community groups with different agendas." TPL had to learn how to sync up land protection with other urgent goals, such as redeveloping a waterfront, creating affordable housing, developing public transit, or revitalizing a neighborhood or city center. In turn, money and other resources for that work might come not just from traditional land-protection sources but from funding for crime prevention, transportation, housing, or urban economic development.

ENGAGING COMMUNITIES

Above all, TPL had to demonstrate that it wasn't a hit-and-run, do-good organization, descending on a neighborhood to impose its own vision of what should happen there, then leaving residents with a park that didn't suit their needs and no framework to

LANDSCAPE ARCHITECTURE 101

Students at the Eighteenth Avenue School in Newark's gritty Central Ward crowd around big sheets of paper, moving colored stickers that represent trees, playground features, and benches: they are helping to design the new Nat Turner Park, guided by landscaping professionals and experts from The Trust for Public Land. In San Francisco's Tenderloin, residents discuss their goals for the renovation of Boedekker Park. In Denver, 50 adults and 30 children show up for the first community meeting to plan an expanded park and garden in East Colfax, a neighborhood of immigrants. And in Watts, Los Angeles, residents attend a series of community workshops to shape the concept for the new Monitor Avenue Park. Reflecting their wishes, the final design includes a playground, a walking path, an exercise area for adults and teens, skate-friendly features, and a grassy lawn with picnic tables.

Since its earliest park projects in the San Francisco Bay Area and Newark, TPL has sought input at the planning stage from the people who would use a park and knew what they wanted from it—whether it be space to garden, play equipment for kids, or shade trees to shelter a picnic. Over the past decade, this well-tested principle of community engagement has evolved into a method that TPL calls "participatory design" and has been put into practice in cities from Seattle to Miami to Atlanta to Santa Fe.

In schools, the process leads to both learning and excitement, as students work with professional planners and landscape designers to transfer ideas into new parks and playgrounds. Melissa Ix, one of the architects involved in a new playground for New York's P.S. 66, described in 2005 what happens: "We basically go through the fundamental building blocks of a typical design process," she said. "We talk about scale, programming, grading, stormwater management, maintenance considerations ..." Students may measure an existing schoolyard to learn how much space is needed for various activities; they may visit other playgrounds or view plans and ideas on a computer.

Decisions must be made: Should a courtyard be dedicated to basketball or quiet activities? What colors should play equipment be? What about balancing the needs of different generations? Kids have endless ideas but sometimes need to be steered toward the possible and practical. Mary Alice Lee, who heads up TPL's NYC Playgrounds Program, recalls that "at P.S. 15, the kids wanted a petting zoo, but happily settled for a wildlife viewing area with birdhouses and a butterfly garden." Meeting the needs of girls as well as boys was creatively solved at P.S. 242 in

Harlem. "It turned out that girls often braided each others' hair in the schoolyard." So the architects came up with a two-level structure where girls could retreat for this activity.

By taking care that parks and playgrounds reflect the character and needs of the communities they serve, TPL's hands-on design process sets up the space for long-term success. And to ensure that community involvement matures into stewardship, TPL looks to partner with strong community groups, land trusts, and active school administrators. "What makes the land valuable," says Andy Stone, NYC Parks for People director, "is the people's ongoing engagement with it, constantly reinvigorating its purpose."

Above: Planning for the renovation of Boeddeker Park in San Francisco. TPL archives. Below: Young landscape architects show off the plans for Mildred Helms Park in Newark, New Jersey. Marni Horwitz.

"What I like about the rebuild process is that TPL did this right. They went to all the stakeholders. That's not the way things have been done here in the past."

—Mike Williams, park neighbor, Boeddeker Park, San Francisco

GUIDING GROWTH

In 1998, Marty Rosen stepped down as The Trust for Public Land's president, though he continued to serve as a valued member of TPL's board of directors. Replacing Marty at the helm was Will Rogers, a Harvard MBA, former Chicago real estate developer, and most recently TPL's western regional director. (He now refers to himself as an "undeveloper.") Under Will's leadership, which continues to this day, TPL has formalized its suite of services, continued to ramp up its work in cities, and in general become more strategic in its approach to conservation. Building on lessons learned during Green Cities, Will grew fond of saying that TPL had to look beyond "emergency room" conservation—sweeping in to save endangered landscapes from the bulldozer. It had to build capacity to help communities use parks and conservation deliberately and proactively to shape a better future.

As the economy began to take off in the mid-1990s, many conservationists and community leaders were alarmed by how quickly open land was being paved over in sprawl development. Whether it was small-scale farms, privately owned woodlands, scenic canyons near expanding towns in the mountain states, or lands bordering urban waterways, many special places that communities had come to regard as public resources were changing hands—their unique character irrevocably changed as well, by a new crop of houses or a shopping mall. As an alternative to sprawl, planning experts focused on a development pattern that had come to be known as "smart growth," which emphasized compact, walkable neighborhoods served by public transit, employment close to home, and a mix of land uses and housing choices.

Now, Will and other TPL leaders suggested that the organization was uniquely positioned to help communities combat sprawl and create what Will called "not simply livable, but lovable communities." TPL proposed that every community should have a conservation "greenprint for growth"—the equivalent of a blueprint for a building. TPL promoted the idea at conferences and presented awards to communities that were modeling the use of proactive conservation to create trails, further economic

Above: The report for TPL's Central Texas Greenprint. Greenprints help plan for conservation in advance of growth. Right: Development around Mountain Island Lake near Charlotte, North Carolina, 1999. Ken Sherman.

development, protect drinking water, and realize other benefits. In partnership with the National Association of Counties, TPL published a four-volume workbook series, *Local Greenprinting for Growth*, detailing how communities can create a conservation vision, secure funding, and acquire land for parks and open space.

At the same time, TPL expanded its conservation tools to help communities address sprawl. It ramped up efforts to help them create dedicated conservation funding sources that would

allow them to conserve land ahead of rapid growth. (See "Follow the Money," page 54.) And it introduced a new "greenprinting" service, which coupled its long-established skills in community engagement with the relatively new geographic information system (GIS) technology.

A greenprint would begin with a community meeting in which residents set out their conservation goals. TPL's GIS experts would then create computerized maps showing what specific landscapes

Historic buildings in Maine's Penobscot River Valley, where TPL's conservation vision team helped local communities and conservationists develop a "green-print" to identify lands for conservation. AJ Whitney.

FOLLOW THE MONEY

"Year in and year out, regardless of political trends, people vote for open space. When asked to vote with their pocketbooks, people understand the value to them personally of protecting open space."

—Michael Scott, Environment Program officer, The William and Flora Hewlett Foundation

Windrush Farm, North Andover, Massachusetts, protected by TPL using funds from that state's Community Preservation Act. Jerry and Marcy Monkman/EcoPhotography.

When The Trust for Public Land was conceiving its nationwide Green Cities Initiative in the early 1990s, the research included surveying city park directors about what they needed to make bigger and better park systems. Recalls Vice President Ernest Cook, who headed up the initiative, "The top four answers were 'Money, money, money, and money.'" It quickly became clear to Cook and his colleagues that "if TPL were to credibly launch a national urban parks initiative, we had to address the issue of funding squarely—gear up a national campaign to generate more funding for urban parks."

That insight—along with withering of federal funding in the 1980s—helped lay the groundwork for what would become TPL's Conservation Finance service, which helps states and communities establish reliable funding streams for parks and conservation. Starting with some of the targeted "Green Cities"—including Los Angeles, Miami, and Seattle's King County—Cook's tiny staff organized major ballot measures that dedicated hundreds of millions for land

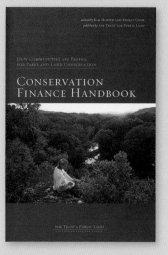

conservation. "We had set a $1.5 billion goal and just blew through that," Cook recalls. "We saw there was no reason to limit this to cities: we could do it in suburban counties and states as well."

Today, TPL's Conservation Finance staff nationwide help states and communities pass tax measures and bond acts by voter initiative to support parks and conservation. They conduct polling, write and test ballot language, develop campaign materials, and help communities single out threatened properties for protection so that voters understand what is at stake in a measure. In 2000, TPL launched an affiliate organization, The Conservation Campaign (TCC), which as a 501(c)(4) nonprofit can support lobbying for ballot measures and legislation.

Through good economic times and bad, voters across the country—and across the political spectrum—have consistently supported such measures, demonstrating the enduring popularity of land conservation. Since 1996, TPL's Conservation Finance service has helped 382 ballot measures gain approval—a success rate of over 80 percent—generating $34 billion in new funding for land conservation. This includes statewide measures in New Jersey, Massachusetts, California, Minnesota, Florida, and other states—particularly powerful because they often include project matching funds for communities that pass their own finance measures. "It's inspiring," says Cook, "because it restores your faith that voters can be trusted to do the right thing if a measure is well planned and well presented."

TPL has also worked to educate the public about conservation finance. In 1994, it began publishing *GreenSense*, a newsletter summarizing achievements and trends in the field nationwide. Then followed a series of yearly LandVote reports on state and ballot results, compiled and published with the Land Trust Alliance, and ultimately the launch of TPL's online LandVote database—a searchable source of information on all conservation funding measures since 1996. In 2004, TPL published the *Conservation Finance Handbook*, which traces the steps to a successful conservation finance measure.

Fly-fishing on the Deschutes River in Bend, Oregon. A 2008 TPL-led greenprint helped identify and prioritize conservation opportunities in fast-growing Deschutes County. Darcy Kiefel.

need to be protected to meet those goals and to assemble what Will Rogers calls "a protected system of parks, trails, watersheds, and working landscapes like farms and forests. That way, as communities grow, they don't lose the places that define their identity." In the decade since this work began, greenprinting has become one of TPL's most powerful conservation tools. "Through greenprinting we can help communities get ahead of the growth curve—and get land conservation out of the emergency room," Will says. (See "Conservation by Computer," page 56.)

PICKING UP TOOLS

Over the same years that The Trust for Public Land has become more strategic, ramped up its work in cities, and added services, it also has been sharpening its founding skill set: conservation real estate transactions. From simple buy-hold-and-sell transactions, TPL elaborated an ever more sophisticated approach to getting lands into public hands.

In the early 1990s, for example, TPL became a banker for the owner of Rutherford Ranch, just east of sprawling San Diego. For decades this 13,000-acre chunk of backcountry was off limits to all but cattle, cowboys, and a few hunters, but now the owner could no longer make payments on a multimillion-dollar loan secured by the property. The only way to pay off the debt was to sell the land—most likely for development. Public agencies savored the ranch's potential for recreation and wildlife habitat, but it would take years to develop the funding required for its protection. So TPL bought the rancher's note from the bank and restructured the debt under the condition that the land would be protected. Over several years, TPL then facilitated the transfer of the ranch to county and state agencies for parks and habitat.

In many ways, this is a classic Trust for Public Land transaction tale. The typical ingredients were all there: a prime piece of land, eager but constrained public agencies, a looming threat of

"Through greenprinting we can help communities get ahead of the growth curve—and get land conservation out of the emergency room."

—Will Rogers, TPL president

CONSERVATION BY COMPUTER

Trust for Public Land GIS director Breece Robertson. Jane Bernard.

[With the greenprint] "we can think parcel by parcel, from the highest peaks to the bottom of Puget Sound.... We can answer questions such as 'What land do we need for salmon?' With this tool you can really see and understand the land."

—Ron Sims, former King County executive

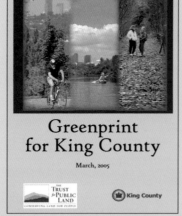

Greenprint for King County

March, 2005

The 2003 King County greenprint was among the first of more than 50 TPL greenprints completed to date in communities nationwide. Right: A GPS device in use along King County's Icy Creek. Dan Lamont.

King County, Washington, spans an area the size of Delaware—from the Cascade Mountains in the east, through evergreen forests cut by rushing snowmelt rivers, to the densely populated coast, including Seattle, and portions of Puget Sound. In addition to nearly 2 million human residents, the county is home to five threatened or endangered species of fish that depend on clean land and water. Its farms and forests are threatened by development. Land needs to be conserved to mitigate flooding, and residents are demanding more parks and trails for recreation.

How do communities like King County decide which lands are most important to protect with limited conservation funds? In 2003, the county asked The Trust for Public Land's Conservation Vision service to complete a computer mapping and community engagement process to set conservation goals and priorities. Since its earliest days, TPL had been talking to communities about those priorities. Now advances in geographical information systems (GIS) have made it possible to display those priorities on sophisticated maps showing lands that might be conserved to protect clean water or scarce farmland, for example, or for trails, habitat, and recreation. Other map layers might indicate where project funding could be available. In 2006, TPL's technology-supported conservation planning process—which it calls "greenprinting"—won a special achievement award from ESRI, the world's leading developer of GIS software.

At the start of a greenprint process, TPL experts hold a series of meetings with stakeholders to set their goals; then data is collected and fed into the computer maps. The last step is usually a detailed interpretive report that serves as a guide to action. A greenprint equips communities to evaluate lands objectively, reach common ground on priorities, and compare current resources with projected growth to reveal future needs. These "living" computer models also can be updated easily as data changes.

"The beauty of using GIS for analysis and modeling is that you can visualize patterns and connections," explains Breece Robertson, director of TPL's Conservation Vision service. "While a two-dimensional map can show that two sections of a trail don't meet, GIS analysis can reveal the obstacles to making

them connect: for example, seasonal runoff or major roads. GIS can also compare alternate scenarios to solve conservation problems."

The King County greenprint, among TPL's most ambitious to date, is one of more than 50 completed by TPL's conservation visioning team over the last decade. Also in Washington State, TPL's greenprint for the Quinault Nation—the first for a sovereign Indian nation—is helping the nation understand not only how its natural and cultural resources might be protected and managed, but also which privately held lands within the reservation's boundary might be restored to tribal control. On the opposite coast, in Maine, 12 Penobscot Valley communities collaborated with TPL on a greenprint to address land use and conservation on a regional scale, identifying the ingredients that sustain the region's quality of life and attract visitors and business. Among other places, TPL has created greenprints for the scenic Litchfield Hills of northwestern Connecticut; fast-growing Douglas County, southeast of Denver; and the Texas hill country near Austin.

Stretching from the Cascade Mountains to Seattle, King County is home to nearly 2 million people. The greenprint helps prioritize lands for conservation. Veronica von Allwörden/Lighthawk.

"Today we have a more robust set of tools than in the past, but everything we are doing is consistent with our original mission—our commitment to the importance of the human-nature connection."

—Will Rogers,
TPL president

loss to private development, and a ticking clock. In its size and complexity, it was also the kind of transaction that few conservation organizations had the resources to take on—the kind that led to a saying around the organization: "There but for TPL …" (would be another lost landscape).

Such projects could be immensely complex and ambitious. In 1998, with support from the David and Lucile Packard Foundation, TPL acquired the third-largest privately owned property on the California coast south of San Francisco—more than 7,000 acres. To do so, the organization had to acquire all assets of the Coast Dairies and Land Company, which had owned the land for more than a century. California state parks wanted part of the land. Part of it was prime agricultural acreage that needed to end up with farmers, and conservationists wanted a hilly interior portion for wildlife habitat. Much of the coastal acreage is now protected as state parkland. And in 2012, most of the inland portion was transferred to the federal Bureau of Land Management. But nearly 15 years after acquiring the massive property, TPL still owns some of the farmland while it works out the details of its protection. In general, TPL does not hold land over the long term; Coast Dairies was an exception to the rule because it really was the only way to preserve a huge chunk of the California coast.

Another conservation technique that evolved over time was the careful crafting of conservation easements that preserve a property's scenic, natural, and recreational values while keeping it in private hands. Often such easements are used to prevent the sale of working farms, ranches, and forests, keeping them in production while stipulating ways the land can and cannot be used: limiting development, for example, or requiring sustainable forestry practices.

TPL has negotiated hundreds of easements, large and small: to preserve oak woodlands on a family ranch near Yosemite National Park, to protect habitat for endangered bats on New Hampshire's Gardner Mountain, to support sustainable forestry and create public access to a big chunk of Wisconsin's Northwoods. In 1988,

TPL and the Land Trust Alliance published *The Conservation Easement Handbook*, the definitive resource on the subject. Updated in 2005, it offers technical guidelines for drafting conservation easements, along with case studies, sample documents, and references to landmark court decisions.

Sometimes the easiest way to meet multiple conservation needs is through a land exchange, such as the complicated ones TPL engineered in New Mexico beginning in 2001. Two Native American pueblos sought to protect cultural sites on land owned by the federal Bureau of Land Management (BLM), while the BLM sought to protect a scenic overlook with sweeping views of the Rio Grande Gorge between Santa Fe and Taos. In several transactions, TPL acquired property for the overlook from a private party and then traded it to the BLM for the land the pueblos wanted.

In another creative land swap, TPL engineered an exchange with no fewer than six key parcels and five landowners to protect for public enjoyment the historic ghost town of Garnet, Montana.

And in northern Maine, TPL conducted delicate negotiations among local groups, state park officials, and conservationist Roxanne Quimby (founder of the Burt's Bees cosmetics empire); Quimby sold 5,000 acres to be opened for recreation, in exchange for land made available elsewhere in the region. A working-forest easement was also part of the deal.

Sometimes an agency wants to make a park but doesn't have funding in place to buy the land. In such cases, TPL may purchase the property and lease it to the agency with an option to buy. Or if funding for a project falls short, TPL may buy a property and split off a small portion for development, using the funds generated to help protect the land with the most conservation value. TPL used this technique in 1988 to create Connecticut's Weir Farm National Historic Site. After working for years to assemble parcels for a park honoring the American impressionist painter Alden Weir, TPL permitted housing development on some of the land (which was already subdivided), while preserving the historic core of the farm.

Page 58: Coastal portions of the 7,000-acre Coast Dairies property were transferred to the California Department of Parks and Recreation. Frank S. Balthis.

THINKING ABOUT MISSION

Why is it important to conserve land for people? Who benefits from new parks and gardens? How does connecting people to land also connect them to a sense of purpose in a changing world? How does conserving land build community as well as personal identity in a diverse society? In short: what values should guide the work of a conservation organization in the 21st century? In the late 1990s, The Trust for Public Land launched the Center for Land and People to examine these questions. As Will Rogers wrote at the time, "We need to view our own good work in the bigger context of being responsible for what actually happens in the world."

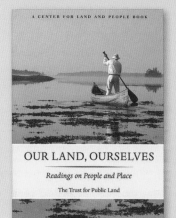

Heading up the effort was Peter Forbes, TPL's former New England director, who'd been doing a lot of thinking about the broader meaning of TPL's work. Traveling the nation as a Trust for Public Land Fellow, Peter collected stories about how TPL projects reinforced the bonds between people and land. And as director of the new center, he conducted workshops that helped TPL staff and the whole conservation community explore the meaning and purpose of conservation. With Peter serving as editor, TPL published a series of four books exploring these topics—anthologies, collections of Peter's own essays, and a handbook for how to tell stories about land and people.

In a parallel effort, TPL reached out to authors who write about people and land, inviting them to join its Stegner Circle of authors, named for the Pulitzer Prize–winning writer and longtime TPL advisor Wallace Stegner. Authors such as Barry Lopez, Peter Matthiessen, Terry Tempest Williams, Tony Hiss, Timothy Egan, David Mas Masumoto, and many others have read at Stegner Circle events in major cities.

In 2005, Peter Forbes left The Trust for Public Land to co-found the Center for Whole Communities, a land-based leadership development organization. But the conversation he helped start at TPL led to a continuing examination of mission. Today every TPL project begins with a formal evaluation of its mission impact in nine areas, such as whether it will strengthen the community, build partnerships, and affirm the connection between land and people.

Peter Forbes. Courtesy Center for Whole Communities.

"Land conservation can help to make people and communities whole."

—Peter Forbes

TPL tore down the Richfield Coliseum south of Cleveland to add the land to the Cuyahoga Valley National Park. *Before:* Janet Century/Heinz Hess. *After:* Ken Sherman.

In response to this galaxy of needs, TPL's urban work coalesced into the Parks for People initiative, a direct descendant of the 1970s Urban Land Program by way of the 1990s Green Cities Initiative.

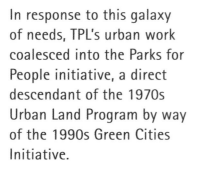

There are many reasons why a public agency chooses to work with TPL rather than protect a parcel directly. A common one is that the land may need to be cleaned up in some way before the agency can assume the legal liabilities associated with ownership. This is often the case when a former industrial property—a so-called "brownfield"—is going to become a park: TPL will clean up the remnants of industrial use before transferring the land to the agency—a process known as remediation. In one notable example, TPL "detoxed" a former railyard near downtown Los Angeles—long known as the "Cornfields" because corn was once grown there—for that city's first state park.

In the most drastic form of remediation, a building must actually be razed before the property can become a park. TPL has done this more often that you might expect: in 1995 a former pen factory was knocked down to add land to Atlanta's Martin Luther King, Jr. National Historic Site. But the largest building TPL ever demolished was certainly the Richfield Coliseum south of Cleveland—once home to the Cleveland Cavaliers basketball team and other sports franchises but no longer in use by 1999. After the stadium was gone, the land was cleaned up, returned to prairie, and added to the Cuyahoga Valley National Park.

TPL's founders might not have imagined that the goal of "pioneering new techniques of land preservation" might one day lead to the razing of a 20,000-seat arena. But, really, why not? "I like to say that we are an organization with opposable thumbs that likes to pick up tools," says TPL president Will Rogers, by which he means not just transaction tools but all the skills that have evolved in TPL's full suite of services. "Today we have a more robust set of tools than in the past," Will adds, "but everything we're doing is completely consistent with our original mission—with that simple powerful commitment to the importance of the human-nature connection. We're still living and breathing that mission 40 years later, and wherever it takes us in the future, I'm sure we'll get there by finding new tools."

PARKS FOR PEOPLE IN THE 21ST CENTURY

In the first days of 2012, The Trust for Public Land celebrated the transfer of 64 New York City community gardens to community land trusts. The event had historical resonance for TPL. For one thing, it was very similar to some of TPL's earliest city work in Oakland and Newark. And TPL had been the owner of these gardens since saving them from the auction block in 1999. Having learned much about what it takes to preserve a crucial urban resource, TPL had spent more than a decade improving the infrastructure of the gardens, raising an endowment to support them, creating land trusts to manage them, and training the gardeners in the practical skills needed to assume ownership.

Entering its fifth decade, TPL remains committed to conserving land from inner city to wilderness, wherever parks and conservation promote human well-being. But as the land-for-people conservation organization, TPL must be particularly engaged in cities and metro areas, where more than 80 percent of the nation's people live.

Never has TPL's expertise in urban parks been needed more. Following a steep downhill slide for cities in the decades following World War II, many Americans are rediscovering the virtues of city life: closeness to their jobs and neighbors; access to cultural resources; the chance to live, work, and play in the same place. Big-city mayors—such as Michael Bloomberg in New York,

IT PAYS TO SAVE

"We were seeing a demand for information at the local level, so we had to start quantifying the benefits project by project and community by community."

—Jessica Sargent-Michaud

In helping communities make the case for parks and conservation, Trust for Public Land staff heard a common refrain: "It's too expensive." To change this perception, people had to see conservation as an investment rather than a luxury—and that meant providing hard information about its economic benefits. Says Vice President Ernest Cook, who helped to pioneer this effort at TPL, "A lot of public money is being invested in parks and conservation, so it seems incumbent on us to be able to understand, interpret, and explain what the payback is. It's part of being accountable."

In the 1990s TPL began to collect and publish summaries of research supporting this case, and it quickly became among the most popular tools on the website. A 1998 report, *The Economic Benefits of Parks and Open Space*, was followed in 2007 by a more comprehensive publication based on commissioned research, *The Economic Benefits of Land Conservation*. That same year, TPL hired a full-time economist, Jessica Sargent-Michaud, to refine the metrics and coordinate work directly with communities. "We were seeing a real demand for this kind of information at the local level," says Sargent. "So we had to start quantifying the benefits project by project and community by community."

That has led to collaborations with community partners around the country and new reports based on specific applications of TPL's research. Reports included the economic benefits from protecting water quality, attracting tourism, enhancing quality of life, improving health, and other factors.

In New Jersey a 2009 TPL report found that every dollar invested in conservation returns $10 in economic benefits— helping convince legislators to put a measure on the ballot to renew that state's successful Green Acres conservation funding program. In Colorado, Sargent found that every dollar the state had invested in ranchland conservation easements had returned $6 in benefits. And in the two counties of Long Island, New York, the team was able to describe $2.74 billion in annual economic benefits.

As in New Jersey, often the research is used to support conservation finance campaigns. "Voters have long recognized the economic benefits of land conservation. They understand that it protects water quality and creates places for children to play," says Sargent. "But decision makers face hard choices and pay attention mainly to dollars-and-cents considerations. This work gives land conservation a seat at the table."

Top: TPL economist Jessica Sargent-Michaud. Andrew Dillon. Above: A TPL report found that Colorado's conservation easements—such as the one protecting the Hutchinson Ranch—returned six dollars for every public dollar invested. Darcy Kiefel.

TPL helped the Chicago Park District expand Haas Park in the park-poor Logan Square neighborhood. Darcy Kiefel.

Cory Booker in Newark, and Rahm Emanuel in Chicago—have launched major park efforts to meet the needs of current residents and to attract new residents and businesses. Civic leaders nationwide are coming to recognize that the quality of urban life depends heavily on investments in the public realm—especially parks. "Parks can and should be regarded as oases for people who live in densely populated environments, Newark's deputy mayor, Stefan Pryor, told *Land&People* magazine in 2007. "We know they are a pivotal component of our social infrastructure."

There is also a growing recognition that close-to-home parks and playgrounds provide a potent antidote to obesity and other diseases linked to the inactivity of modern life. Health experts (and more recently, First Lady Michelle Obama's Let's Move! campaign) have called attention to rising rates of obesity—especially troubling in children—due to poor diets and lack of exercise. And today's children lack opportunities to play in and experience the outdoors, as highlighted by journalist Richard Louv in his bestselling book, *Last Child in the Woods: Saving Our Children from Nature-Deficit Disorder*. Increasingly, city parks, playgrounds, and trails are seen as ways to stem the rising tide of diabetes and heart disease along with spiraling health-care costs. (See "Parks for Health," page 64.)

In response to this galaxy of needs, in 2005 TPL's urban work coalesced into the Parks for People initiative, a direct descendant of the 1970s Urban Land Program by way of the 1990s Green Cities Initiative. The work involves all TPL services—from Conservation Visioning to Park Design and Development—working toward a common goal: to put a park, a playground, or a natural area within a ten-minute walk of every American home.

While TPL has helped create showplace downtown parks in cities such as Seattle, Santa Fe, and Los Angeles, much of today's Parks for People work is taking place in the neighborhoods, where parks offer the closest recreation and connection to nature. In some cities, as many as two-thirds of children lack access to a neighborhood park or natural area. TPL is hard at work on neighborhood park projects in New York, where it has created more than 200 parks, playgrounds, gardens, and natural areas, and transformed more than 150 asphalt schoolyards into community parks. In San Francisco, TPL is completely refurbishing three neighborhood parks, including one in the rough-and-tumble Tenderloin. Another is only three blocks from Koshland Park, site of TPL's first San Francisco park project nearly 40 years earlier.

Recently TPL dedicated a new park in Maywood, California, the most densely settled city west of the Mississippi, with more parks on the drawing board in Los Angeles County, as well as green spaces in neighborhood alleyways. Also in L.A, TPL has developed more than two dozen outside exercise areas in city parks as part of its Fitness Zones® program, which is now expanding to Miami, other Florida,

and elsewhere. Featuring all-weather workout gear, Fitness Zones hold great promise for reducing obesity and diseases related to inactivity among people who can't afford membership fees at private gyms.

In Chicago, TPL is taking a major role in the creation of The Bloomingdale—a three-mile-long park and trail on an abandoned elevated rail corridor that will bring new recreation and open space to four densely settled neighborhoods. In Atlanta, a 2005 TPL report helped build momentum for the BeltLine, a 26-mile greenway around downtown. In New Orleans, TPL undertook a major effort to help rebuild the much-loved City Park after Hurricane Katrina and now is working on a new greenway and the city's first new park since that storm. TPL park projects are also under way in Minneapolis, Denver, and Philadelphia, among other cities.

As the only major conservation organization focused on cities, TPL has sought to collect and share research about the nature and benefits of city parks. One goal is to make parks stand out among many priorities for municipal governments and to compete successfully for private or public funding. Leading this research is the Center for City Park Excellence (CCPE), established in 2001 and based in Washington, D.C. The center is headed by Peter Harnik,

Above: Celebrating the opening of the TPL-refurbished Hayes Valley Playground in San Francisco. Pat Mazzera Photography. Left: Student musicians perform at the dedication of their new playground at P.S. 164, Borough Park, Brooklyn, New York. Naomi Ellenson.

PARKS FOR HEALTH

"[People] desperately need parks that are located, designed, built, and programmed in a way that allows them to integrate activity and exercise into their daily lives."

—Peter Harnik, director, TPL's Center for City Park Excellence

Top: A woman jogs along a St. Petersburg, Florida, rail trail created with TPL's help. Darcy Kiefel.

Looking into The Trust for Public Land's future, Will Rogers sees much of its work taking place "at the intersection of public health and nature—the relationship of parks and open space and health." It's no secret that health issues related to inactivity, such as obesity and diabetes, are on the rise, especially among children. And there's growing recognition that well-used parks and open space can help address the problem. Research shows that outdoor play is vital for healthy child development, social and emotional as well as physical.

TPL is applying its decades of parks experience and research to a broad range of efforts to better Americans' health. A big first step is improving access to parks, via TPL's goal of putting a park within a ten-minute walk of all Americans through active Parks for People programs in New York, Newark, Los Angeles, Chicago, San Francisco, Philadelphia, and other cities. Another is to reshape or reoutfit parks to meet the needs of today's park users, especially for exercise. In one of its most promising efforts to promote health,

TPL is partnering with foundations and local parks districts to install Fitness Zones—outdoor exercise areas fitted with isometric workout gear—in existing parks. TPL and its partners have installed 30 of these systems in Los Angeles and several Florida communities, and TPL is working to spread the program nationwide.

But to advance health as much as possible, parks also need to be well used, says Peter Harnik, director of The Trust for Public Land's Center for City Park Excellence (CCPE). "It's not enough to just tell people to go exercise," he says. "There are so many variables in the way parks are situated, managed, and programmed." So TPL has sought to pinpoint the factors that encourage or discourage use. A recent CCPE report, *From Fitness Zones to the Medical Mile: How Urban Park Systems Can Best Promote Health and Wellness*, highlights ways to increase park usage for maximum health—everything from increasing health-related programming to reducing stress by calming traffic in parks.

"It's not enough to just tell people to go exercise. There are so many variables in the way parks are situated, managed, and programmed. Some park systems do a better job than others."

—Peter Harnik, director, TPL's Center for City Park Excellence

author of several books on city parks. CCPE's long-term report series, City Park Facts, is the leading source of data on park systems in the nation's 100 largest cities—an indispensable tool for planners, decision makers, and park advocates. "Using our data, if you take a trip to Boston or Minneapolis and like what you see, you can compare what your city has with them—everything from acreage to playgrounds to recreation centers to swimming pools," Peter says. In partnership with the City Park Alliance, the research team also manages the City Parks Blog, offering up-to-date information on city parks, and produces in-depth reports on the economic benefits that a city's park system brings to a city. (See "Parks at the Center," page 67.)

More recently TPL launched a new website to help cities determine where parks are most needed. The Trust for Public Land ParkScore™ Project provides an overview of how well 40 city park systems offer close-to-home parks, as well as each system's level of investment in park services. The website offers dynamic maps and information that will help park leaders improve park systems. Underlying the new website are CCPE's data on park services from City Park Facts and new park access maps from TPL's award-winning GIS program. (See "Scoring City Parks," page 69.)

Jamie Hoyte, who recently retired after more than 15 years on TPL's national board of directors, has been eloquent in urging the organization to firmly stake out its urban territory. "The trust has not only stayed true to its early focus on urban communities but has built on that over the years," he says with pride. "The big recent evolution I see is our increased recognition that we can and should sharpen our focus on urban work, talk about it in an even more robust way." He adds, "Other national groups have begun working in cities, in their specialized areas, but our long history of expertise gives TPL preeminence."

Trust for Public Land Fitness Zones offer everyone a chance to stay in shape—including people who can't afford membership in a private gym. The outdoor exercise areas are already installed in 30 public parks in Los Angeles, and the program is now expanding to Florida and other states. Rich Reid Photography.com.

Atlanta's first skate park is a popular feature of the new Historic Fourth Ward Park, created with TPL's help and opened in 2011. Darcy Kiefel.

The big goals remain as ever: conserving places of community importance, creating ways to experience close-to-home nature, and forging mutually beneficial bonds between land and people.

THE PERSISTENCE OF INNOVATION

In the years to come, because of The Trust for Public Land, Americans will be able to:

- Launch a kayak or rowing shell from the Cleveland Rowing Foundation's new boathouse on the Cuyahoga River.

- Pick up a box of fresh vegetables from the Community Supported Agriculture program at Crimson and Clover Farm in Northampton, Massachusetts.

- Stroll on The Bloomingdale, a three-mile-long park and trail on a former elevated rail line in Chicago.

- Take a dip in newly protected Volcano Lake in the shadow of California's Sierra Buttes.

- Execute an exhilarating "ollie" or "grind" at a new skateboard park in Atlanta.

- Bike the Rollercoaster or other challenging trails at Millstone Hill, a former granite quarry being reborn as a Vermont community forest.

- Explore an old-growth hardwood forest in Congaree National Park, South Carolina.

- Relax, breathe deep, picnic, or play at new community parks and playgrounds built in partnership with the city of Philadelphia.

These are a few of the projects The Trust for Public Land has completed recently or will be working on in the years just ahead. The big goals remain as ever: conserving places that are important to American communities, creating ways for people to experience nature close to home, forging bonds between land and people to their mutual benefit. The range of TPL's work will likely embrace what we've seen so far—meeting the demand for green space and recreation in dense cities and the growing communities around

PARKS AT THE CENTER

A peek inside the latest City Park Facts report yields all kinds of fascinating factoids. What's the biggest urban park in the nation? (Chugach State Park in Anchorage, at 490,125 acres.)

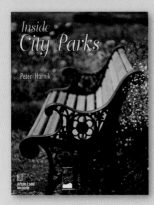

What's the oldest city park? (Plaza de la Constitución in St. Augustine, Florida.) What park gets the most visits? (New York's Central Park, with 35 million annually.) Where will you find the most playgrounds per capita? (Madison, Wisconsin.) What parks have the most basketball hoops, off-leash dog parks, baseball diamonds, or swimming pools per capita? It's all here. Published annually and based on a survey of the nation's 100 largest park and recreation systems, City Park Facts is an indispensable resource for city planners and promoters, journalists, and park advocates making the case for park funding based on hard facts and figures.

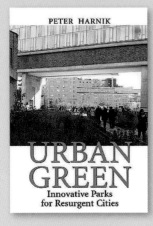

But City Park Facts is only the best-known product of The Trust for Public Land's Center for City Park Excellence, which since its founding in 2001 has become a leading source of information and research on city parks and park systems nationwide. Headquartered in Washington, D.C., and directed by noted park expert Peter Harnik, the center publishes widely on the economic and health benefits of parks and on the best practices for planning, creating, managing, and paying for parks. In partnership with the City Parks Alliance, the center also publishes the City Parks Blog, a leading online source of park news and information (cityparksblog.org).

Since 2007, the center has helped more than a dozen cities measure the positive economic impact of their park systems in increased property taxes, profits from tourism, reduced health care costs, and the value of natural services performed by parks, such as stormwater management and reduced air pollution.

"We need great city parks to keep the hearts of our communities beating," Peter Harnik says. "Parks are the publicly available places city dwellers can go to enjoy the outdoors, stay in shape, and recharge their souls."

"We need great city parks to keep the hearts of our communities beating."

—Peter Harnik

Top: Peter Harnik. Andrew Harnik.
Below: Children explore a sign for Gold Medal Park in Minneapolis. Darcy Kiefel.

"From the beginning there was a commitment to come up with new ways of carrying out the mission."

—Will Rogers,
TPL president

them; protecting land that supports healthy forests and watersheds; working with multiple partners on big, landscape-scale projects in the wide open spaces, to the benefit of people, wild things, and the natural systems that sustain us all.

The need will be greater than ever. Cities and suburbs won't stop expanding (or getting more crowded). Park infrastructure will reach its natural life span and need renewing, while the needs of park users evolve. The health challenges that stem from our mostly sedentary lifestyles will multiply. Clean and sufficient water supplies for drinking and irrigation will become scarcer—a problem as urgent as finding new energy sources, many believe. Living in an ever-more technologically complex society will intensify our need for the refreshment and relief found in nature. And our emerging understanding of the looming climate crisis demands conservation solutions across the entire nationscape where TPL works. (See "Conservation for a Cooler Future," page 70.)

But the real lesson of the past is that we don't know just what the future will bring. This is where the character of an organization is revealed. Its founders didn't foresee that The Trust for Public Land would be running ballot campaigns, or mapping natural resources on computers, or helping American landscapes adjust

to a warming climate. What they did understand—and designed into the DNA of the organization—is that flexibility and innovation would enable TPL to adapt to profound changes in the economic, social, political, environmental, and technological matrix in which it operates. "The original vision was simple and powerful," says Will Rogers. "It was about the value of our human connection with nature wherever that can happen. And the other principle from the beginning was a commitment to come up with new ways of carrying out that mission."

TPL came into being because Huey Johnson wanted to try something new with legal and financial tools being developed by conservationists in the 1970s. But that was not enough for Huey and his cohorts. Realizing that change is inevitable—even desirable—they set forth as a founding goal "pioneering new techniques of conservation and funding that can be used as models nationwide." The founders' embrace of the new has persisted through 40 years of solving conservation problems. Is the deal too tough? Let's think of another way to do it. Do communities need money for conservation? Let's figure out how to help them raise it. How can we create parks in cities where there is little or no parkland? How can we use land conservation to protect drinking water? And so on. TPL has been an organization powered by such questions, always in search of new conservation solutions.

Will Rogers sees TPL more and more becoming a "thought leader" in land conservation. "I think we're now engaged in raising awareness of the importance of what we're doing and the assets we bring to it," he says. If he had to pick one theme around which TPL's work in the near future might gather, "it's probably at the intersection of public health and nature—the relationship of parks and open

Right: Congaree National Park, South Carolina, created with TPL's help in seven projects over almost 20 years. Darcy Kiefel. Below: Children play in Volcano Lake in California's Sierra Nevada, protected in 2011. Rich Reid Photography.com.

SCORING CITY PARKS

How does your city's park system compare with others in how well it serves residents? Launched in 2012, The Trust for Public Land's ParkScore™ Project is designed to answer that question. The project website at parkscore.tpl.org provides a quick comparison—systems are rated at one to four "park benches"—along with in-depth maps to help park professionals understand how a system can better serve residents and where parks are needed most. The website kicked off with ratings and maps for the nation's 40 largest cities.

Ratings are based on the percentage of residents living within a half-mile (ten-minute) walk of a park, the median size of a city's parks, the amount of parkland related to population, and the services and investment in the park system. Underlying the rating system are data on these and other factors collected by TPL's Center for City Park Excellence as well as geographic information system (GIS) data gathered by TPL's Conservation Vision team.

The groundbreaking interactive maps allow park professionals and other users to zoom in and study park access block by block. And the maps are "smart" enough to base ten-minute access not only on the distance between parks and residents, but also on the location of park entrances and whether the route to the park might be blocked by physical obstacles such as a major highway. The website also provides access information about each public park in every one of the 40 cities.

"You can't have a great city without a great park system. We hope that ParkScore inspires cities to focus on parks, and we're eager to work with cities to help them build the best park systems imaginable."

—Christopher Kay,
TPL executive vice president

CONSERVATION FOR A COOLER FUTURE

"The natural question for us was: 'What's land got to do with it?' Today we're realigning much of our work to address the climate challenge."

—Jad Daley, director, TPL Climate Conservation Program

Decades ago, a vast swath of northeastern Louisiana was cleared for farming. Once known as the "American Amazon," this region of oxbow lakes and bottomland hardwoods is now protected in part by the 80,000-acre Tensas River National Wildlife Refuge. Here, The Trust for Public Land and its partners have planted trees in an effort to capture more than 3 million tons of carbon dioxide from the atmosphere over the next 70 years. That's like taking 626,000 cars and light trucks off the road for a year.

"As people began looking for climate change solutions, the natural question for us was: 'What's land got to do with it?'" says Jad Daley, director of TPL's Climate Conservation Program. "Today we're realigning much of our work to address the climate challenge." For example, Daley says, "TPL's Conservation Vision team is creating a new GIS mapping tool to identify lands with the greatest potential to absorb carbon."

Often referred to as "climate mitigation," planting trees and conserving carbon-rich forestlands to "sequester" CO_2 from the atmosphere is one of three approaches taken by TPL's program. The second is all about adaptation: conserving watersheds and other natural lands that will help people as well as wildlife adjust to a changing climate. Adaptation efforts often focus on the conservation of large or interconnected landscapes, so that wildlife can shift locations as the climate changes. This is an important goal of TPL's work in the Midwest's Northwoods, the Connecticut River Valley, the Northern Rockies, the Northern Sierra, and other locations.

Third, TPL is working to address the climate crisis by using parks, trails, and greenways to help create compact, more energy-efficient, climate-smart communities. Greenways and trails support nonmotorized transportation, reducing greenhouse gas emissions. And great parks serve as the communal backyards for more compact communities. Natural parks—especially wooded ones—also cool the air in their immediate vicinity, capture small amounts of CO_2, and absorb stormwater to help prevent flooding.

TPL's Conservation Vision team helps cities develop a climate plan that includes a strong role for parks, greenways, and other natural areas. Project staff helps implement those plans, and Conservation Finance helps fund them.

Above: Jad Daley. Tim Coburn Photo.com.
Right: The Connecticut River watershed is a target landscape for TPL climate adaptation efforts. Jerry and Marcy Monkman/EcoPhotography.

"An old lady talking to her houseplants, a weekend gardener planting marigolds among his carrots and spinach, and a backpacker exultantly surveying a wilderness to whose highest point he has just won, are all on the same wavelength."

—Wallace Stegner, former TPL advisor

space and health." By this he means not just physical health, though that's where so much current attention revolves, but also a healthy environment, healthy communities, and a healthy economy.

It's the kind of big-picture thinking that gets former president and current board member Marty Rosen excited about TPL's future. "I think we are coming to stress this concept of the 'four H's,' as I call it," he says, referring to the several kinds of health. "When TPL embraces in a coherent fashion all that this covers—from biological diversity to health and fitness to transportation and jobs—we offer a unique, holistic enterprise that most thoughtful people would like to be part of, and should be invited to participate in even more fully." And that participation should be not just emotional, but also financial, Marty believes.

Chief Philanthropy Officer Margie Kim Bermeo agrees. "Philanthropy is the currency that moves the mission forward," she says.

"So much work needs to be done, and philanthropy gives us the means to do it much more quickly."

No one knows what the future will bring or how we will ultimately fulfill a vision in which all Americans enjoy access to parks and protected lands near where they live. But one way or another, it starts with big thinking. "Whether it's a national park or a playground close to home, we should be thinking about the full range of connections with the natural world—with our food sources, or where our water comes from, or where we get our dose of fresh air," Will Rogers says. "A lot of organizations are focused on one thing or the other: on wilderness or watersheds or biodiversity. I think the genius of The Trust for Public Land's founders was to say: we're focused on people and all their connections with nature through the land. And that will take us where we need to go."

Landmarks—
Innovation in Action

EVERY MOUNTAINSIDE PROTECTED, EVERY CITY PARK created by The Trust for Public Land is not only a place to be enjoyed by generations of Americans but also an event in the organization's evolving history. So each "landmark" in this part of the book is both a treasured piece of landscape and a notable moment in time. With nearly 4,500 conservation projects completed and hundreds of parks, gardens, and playgrounds created nationwide, The Trust for Public Land does not lack for landmarks. By rough measure, the ones cataloged in the following pages represent only 1 or 2 percent of the organization's accomplishments over the last 40 years, during which time it averaged one conservation project completed every other business day. It was hard to choose which ones to include, and downright painful to decide which ones must be left out. Every place we protect, every park we create, is a landmark to the people who use it and love it. These then are landmarks among landmarks, offered as a sample of The Trust for Public Land's work over its first 40 years.

Sabbathday Lake Shaker Village, Maine, protected in 2007.
Jerry and Marcy Monkman/EcoPhotography.

PARKS FOR PEOPLE

Since its founding, The Trust for Public Land has become the nation's leader among nonprofits in creating parks and conserving land in and around cities, where more than 80 percent of Americans live. In some cities, as many as two in three residents do not have access to a nearby park, playground, or open space. As a result, an entire generation is growing up without a connection to nature, missing out on the daily chances for recreation, exercise, community building, and renewal that parks provide. The Trust for Public Land believes that every American—in particular, every child—should live within a ten-minute walk of a park, playground, or natural area. Well-maintained parks and playgrounds reduce crime, revitalize local economies, and bring neighborhoods together. They also promote public health, lowering a community's collective risk of obesity, diabetes, and other disorders linked to inactivity. To date, The Trust for Public Land has created or protected more than one thousand parks, natural areas, greenways, and community gardens—boosting local economies and improving the quality of life nationwide.

Lake Eola Park, Orlando, Florida, is being enlarged with TPL's help. Darcy Kiefel.

OLYMPIC SCULPTURE PARK

"With the opening of SAM's Olympic Sculpture Park, Seattle at last gets a major downtown public space to match its ambitions as a city."

—Trevor Body,
The Seattle Times, May 17, 2010

Working with the Seattle Art Museum, The Trust for Public Land helps create a showplace park on the last undeveloped piece of Seattle's waterfront.

WHERE: Seattle, Washington

YEARS: 1998–2007

HIGHLIGHTS

- In 1999, The Trust for Public Land acquires a 7.3-acre former oil tank farm zoned for development; later a third parcel was added to bring the park site to 8.5 acres.
- The Seattle Art Museum and TPL jointly raise $16.5 million to purchase the site.
- Seattle's leading corporations and private donors make major gifts to create the park and endow its long-term maintenance.

SIDELIGHT
A living sculpture commissioned for the park contains a Douglas fir "nurse log" emblematic of the Pacific Northwest ecosystem.

Surrounded as it is by natural wonders, the city of Seattle is surprisingly light on world-class urban parks. By the time this dawned on civic leaders, real estate had become so valuable that it was hard to foresee how any large new public space could happen. Which makes the creation of the Olympic Sculpture Park even more remarkable.

The creation story itself is extraordinary. During a fly-fishing trip to Mongolia in the mid-1990s, then Trust for Public Land national board member Martha Wyckoff fell into conversation with Mimi Gates, director of the Seattle Art Museum (and married to Bill Gates Sr., father of the Microsoft

> "This site will connect Seattle's past and future, just as it connects art and open space."
>
> —Martha Wyckoff,
> TPL board member emeritus

Pages 76–77: The Olympic Sculpture Park on opening day. Benjamin Benschneider. Right: The park site before renovation. Scott Areman. *Below: The Eagle by Alexander Calder, silhouetted against Puget Sound.* Benjamin Benschneider.

founder). The museum was concerned, Gates confided, that many important large works of sculpture owned by Seattle residents could be scattered to other cities if the museum couldn't acquire them, so it hoped to build a sculpture park. But where in this crowded city? Said Martha, "I know an organization that might be able to help with that."

Soon Martha and staff project manager Chris Rogers began roaming the city looking for possible sites. The most promising was a spacious but dismal lot overlooking the Elliot Bay waterfront just north of downtown, where the UNOCAL company had been storing oil for decades. Even after cleanup, the land didn't look like much: two barren fenced parcels divided by a major roadway. But the views across Puget Sound were glorious, and the site would become glorious, too, with enough vision and money.

Martha recalls the passionate and productive collaboration of the two partners: on fundraising, site planning, the works. "The Trust for Public Land wanted to connect public access to open space with core civic values. The museum wanted to reach out to the green/outdoors community. This project brought those communities together in an amazing partnership—we shared rolodexes and friends, put together committees that didn't look like either organization. And the results were spectacular."

After negotiating a six-month option on the land—keeping condo and hotel developers at bay—TPL worked with the museum to raise the $16.5 million needed to buy it, completing the transaction in 1999. Before work began, a third parcel was added, right on the bay, and the final innovative design by New York's Weiss/Manfredi architectural firm knit the three parcels into a Z-shaped park that bridged both the highway and a set of railway tracks.

On any day now in Seattle, thousands of people stroll through the 8.5-acre sculpture park, taking in works by some of the world's leading artists: Alexander Calder, Anthony Caro, Mark Di Suvero, Ellsworth Kelly, Richard Serra, and Tony Smith. They can traverse roadways and railroad tracks on quiet paths and landscaped bridges. They can experience a sampling of the Northwest bioregion in the park's natural features, including restored salmon habitat along the bay, and drink in the sweeping views.

And they can take a break on a terrace named for The Trust for Public Land, in honor of a partnership that began on a river in Mongolia.

GWYNNS FALLS TRAIL

More than a decade in the making, an urban greenway provides recreation, links neighborhoods, and serves as a catalyst for change.

WHERE: Baltimore, Maryland

YEARS: 1992–2005

HIGHLIGHTS
- The Gwynns Falls Trail links some 30 neighborhoods with 8 parks that total about 2,000 acres.
- To supplement public dollars for the ambitious greenway project, The Trust for Public Land raises $3 million from private donors, including the Baltimore Orioles.
- The trail provides space for a free after-school program for kids and opportunities for all residents to walk, bike, and kayak the stream.
- One branch of the trail ends at the Inner Harbor, another at the Middle Branch of the Patapsco River, where it is helping to revive an urban backwater.

SIDELIGHT
Part of the trail runs along a historic carriage path and under the nation's oldest continuously operating railroad bridge.

Start in 1904, when civic leaders hired the famous Olmsted Brothers to design spacious public parks around Baltimore's major streams, including the rocky, forest-fringed Gwynns Falls. Fast-forward to the 1970s, when neighborhoods along the stream were sunk in poverty, and the woods were deemed too dangerous to visit. Move on to 1991, when The Trust for Public Land and civic leaders began to imagine a trail along Gwynns Falls, with, in the words of then TPL field representative Chris Rogers, "kids from the neighborhoods being able to bike down to the Inner Harbor … or tourists being able to discover a trail that will lead them to a forest in the middle of the city." Then cut to June 2005, when the Gwynns Falls Trail opened—a 14-mile chain of hike-and-bike paths connecting a dozen parks and playgrounds, with historic and natural sites along the stream, and a final segment reaching downtown and Baltimore's showplace waterfront.

It took more than a decade of work by The Trust for Public Land and many partners—including the city and two successive mayors, the Baltimore Parks & People Foundation, and civic and business groups—to reach this happy outcome. TPL commissioned a master plan and gathered community input, raised $3 million in private funding for the $14 million project, acquired a dozen privately owned parcels to fill in the missing links on the greenway, and helped restore greenway parks. The newly created Leon Day Park, named for a hometown star of Negro League baseball, is now a sports destination for the whole city. Where the stream once divided neighborhoods, today the trail knits them together. It offers access to nature for people living in park-poor areas and promotes healthy recreation for all Baltimoreans.

Above: Young football players in Leon Day Park along the Gwynns Falls Trail. Steffi Graham. *Below: Enjoying a wooded portion of the trail.* Steffi Graham.

"The trail is a shining example of how strong partnerships can enhance our environment and improve our quality of life."

—Kimberly Flowers, former director, Baltimore Recreation and Parks

BRUCE VENTO NATURE SANCTUARY

"Creating the park has particularly made a difference for young people, who have been very involved—removing invasive plants, reforesting with native species, serving as ambassadors for the sanctuary."

—Carol Carey,
Lower Phalen Creek Project

Neighbors unite across cultures to reclaim a 30-acre industrial site for a close-to-home urban natural area near the Mississippi River.

WHERE: Saint Paul, Minnesota

YEARS: 2001–2008

HIGHLIGHTS

• Nestled at the foot of tall sandstone bluffs, the sanctuary preserves historic caves, natural springs, and remnants of the area's industrial past.
• The Trust for Public Land leads the transaction and finance work, but the vision is driven by the community.
• Visitors can walk, bike, watch wildlife, or just enjoy a surprisingly secluded bit of nature a few minutes from downtown.

SIDELIGHT

In 2005, the park campaign won a national award from Take Pride in America, which recognizes volunteer efforts on behalf of public lands.

"It's extraordinary that a group of neighbors looked at a piece of abused and neglected land and decided to do something about it. The Trust for Public Land helped them make this park what it is: a permanent celebration of the power of community." The speaker is Sue Vento, widow of the late U.S. Representative Bruce Vento of Minnesota, whose favorite work as a longtime member of Congress was expanding the nation's parks—and for whom this special Saint Paul park is named.

Dedicated in 2005, the nearly 30-acre park lies just east of downtown Saint Paul, between the Mississippi River and lofty sandstone bluffs, in the former floodplain of Phalen Creek and Trout Brook. Prehistoric Hopewell people built burial mounds on these bluffs, and the land is still revered by their Dakota descendants—especially a sacred site they call Wakan Tipi and that became known as Carver's Cave. European immigrants later settled below the bluffs, sharing space with the sawmills, breweries, and other industries that employed them, and eventually railroads took over most of the land.

Above: Visitors to Carver's Cave, 1875. Courtesy Minnesota Historical Society. *Right: The new nature sanctuary occupies a former railyard along the Mississippi River.* Sarah Clark/Lower Phalen Creek Project.

By the time neighborhood groups began eyeing it for a park, the railyard had become a contaminated brownfield—which didn't deter the neighbors, who worked for years to win support from the city, county, state, and federal representatives. "We walked around, pushed through, leaped over obstacles—any way we could keep it moving forward," recalled Carol Carey, chair of the Lower Phelan Creek Project, a nonprofit dedicated to using parks and trails to strengthen St. Paul's blue-collar East Side and Lowertown neighborhoods. The Trust for Public Land helped navigate the legal, financial, and political maze; rounded up public and private financing; and negotiated the land's purchase with the railway.

Creating the sanctuary was a labor of love on the part of the diverse communities that now use it. Some of the latest wave of immigrants, Hmong people from Southeast Asia, have been active in efforts to restore the abused land, as have the local Dakota people. Nonhuman residents and visitors benefit too: the park provides habitat for migratory waterfowl and songbirds along the Mississippi Flyway.

Most of all it's become a place for today's residents and future generations to experience nature close to the city. "When I see all the walkers strolling, artists painting, and families playing here, I know Bruce would have been proud to have his name associated with it," Sue Vento says.

Local teen volunteers clear invasive plants.
Darcy Kiefel.

"It's not just about owning the land. It's about fostering strong groups that manage community assets. We're building a network of permanent community open space."

—Andy Stone, director,
TPL Parks for People–New York City

Top: Sherman Avenue Community Garden, South Bronx. Catherine Wint. Above: Tremont Community Garden, Bronx. Ken Sherman.

The Trust for Public Land rescues scores of community gardens from the auction block—then trains their gardeners to undertake permanent ownership.

WHERE: New York, New York

YEARS: 1978–present

HIGHLIGHTS

• TPL begins supporting New York's community gardens after opening its New York office in 1978.

• In 1999, TPL steps in to save 62 of gardens on city-owned land from being auctioned for development.

• Over a decade, TPL invests $4 million in garden improvements, establishes three borough-based land trusts, and trains the gardeners to take ownership of the land.

SIDELIGHT

In the wake of the 9/11 attacks, gardeners from the 6th and B Garden on the Lower East Side rally to help clean up Ground Zero.

"The gardens must be saved!" Shouting this battle cry was a man dressed as a sunflower, climbing a gingko tree outside New York's City Hall. It was 1999, boom times for real estate, and Mayor Giuliani's government wanted to capitalize on the rising value of many city-owned lots that had been vacated in more dismal days. But among the lots on the auction block were dozens of community gardens that residents had tended for 20 years or more. Not about to be uprooted, many gardeners rallied in protest. The Trust for Public Land, their ally through the decades, negotiated hard with the city, desperately raised funds, and in the end pulled off an eleventh-hour rescue, acquiring 62 of the gardens at risk. (Later acquisitions brought the number to 69.)

But TPL didn't just buy the gardens. "We embarked on a process with neighborhoods to help ensure the gardens' permanence, long-term stewardship, and importance in a network of New York City public open space," said Andy Stone, director of TPL's Parks for People–New York City program. The ultimate goal was for the

Acquiring 69 gardens all at once, though, was a big jump in scale. Never intending to hold on to the gardens, Parks for People—New York set about helping them grow roots so they could stand on their own. With support from its donors, TPL invested more than $4 million in new water systems, fences, and sidewalks for the gardens—and worked with garden groups to build their capacity for leadership and organizing. Most important, TPL took the legal steps to create the new land trusts. The process took more than a decade, but over the last few years TPL has transferred most of the gardens to the land trusts.

With the recent trend toward locally grown, healthier food, more and more of New York's gardeners are bringing produce home to their families, giving it to charities, or selling it at farmers' markets. Of all the gardens' blessings, it's hard to say which tops the list, but to many it's the social capital residents harvest from them. The gardens are credited with bringing down crime, creating stability, raising property values, and uniting neighbors around a shared endeavor—especially in the new land trust framework. "As a model of ownership among folks who don't own anything, let alone land, it's empowering," said Ethan Winter of the Land Trust Alliance, which worked with TPL to train the land trusts. "It's one thing to grow your food in the garden you love. It's another thing to know your organization owns it."

"Once you open that gate, it's like a flytrap. Everybody starts coming in. 'Can we have a party?' they ask. 'Can we have a barbecue?'"

—Maria Rodriguez,
Sherman Avenue Community Garden

Left: A young gardener at Classon Ful-Gate Block Association Garden, Brooklyn. Seth Sherman. *Below: A community fish fry at the Euclid/Pine Street Block Association Garden, Brooklyn.* Marni Horwitz.

gardeners to own and control their garden plots. To that end, TPL organized and trained leadership for three borough-wide land trusts in Manhattan, Brooklyn-Queens, and the Bronx—together forming the nation's largest urban land trust.

The community gardening movement germinated in Manhattan's Lower East Side, where in the 1970s residents began to till plots on land the city owned but ignored. It spread quickly through New York's boroughs, each garden reflecting its neighborhood character and ethnic mix—from Pleasant Village Garden in Spanish Harlem to the 1100 Bergen Street Garden in Brooklyn's Crown Heights to the Garden of Happiness in the South Bronx. They became the city's front porches and backyards—places where stressed urbanites could relax in a tranquil setting, meet neighbors, play, grow produce, and gather for summer cookouts. They attracted support from private nonprofits and city agencies. And they found a dedicated partner in The Trust for Public Land. Since setting up shop in New York in 1978, TPL helped raise funds to buy space for gardens, worked with community groups to build and maintain them, and arranged to transfer some gardens to the parks department for protection.

CAHUENGA PEAK

"It's like saying let's build a house in the middle of Yellowstone Park. There are some things that are more important. The Hollywood Sign represents the dreams of millions. It's a symbol. It is as the Eiffel Tower is to Paris. It represents the movies."

—Hugh Hefner

After leading a successful fundraising campaign, The Trust for Public Land protects the backdrop of the iconic Hollywood Sign.

WHERE: Los Angeles, California

YEARS: 2009–2012

HIGHLIGHTS
* Local conservationists and officials seek to protect the land behind the Hollywood Sign: 138 acres on Cahuenga Peak once owned by Howard Hughes.
* In 2009, TPL secures an option on the land at a reduced price, staving off development of luxury homes.
* To kick off the fundraising, TPL wraps the sign with a banner reading "SAVE THE PEAK."
* With strong support from the whole community, Cahuenga Peak is added to Griffith Park in 2012.

SIDELIGHT
The biggest obstacle to wrapping the Hollywood Sign was the size of the sign itself—like wrapping nine five-story buildings standing side by side.

An icon of fame and fortune, the Hollywood Sign daily reminds residents and visitors to Los Angeles of the dream embodied in the busy streets below. For a few days in February 2010, those who looked up saw the sign transformed into a beacon for conservation, its huge letters now reading "SAVE THE PEAK." Covered by media outlets worldwide and carried live via a cnn.com web feed, the wrapping of the Hollywood Sign broadcast a once-in-a-lifetime opportunity to conserve Cahuenga Peak—a rare expanse of open space in the heart of the Southern California megalopolis that serves as the sign's natural backdrop.

Offering sweeping views across the L.A. basin, Cahuenga Peak was once owned by billionaire industrialist and movie producer Howard Hughes, who planned to build a lofty love nest there for his then girlfriend Ginger Rogers. The house was never built (Rogers broke off the relationship), and the 138-acre parcel eventually was acquired by a development group that in 2008 won the rights to build four luxury homes on it. The land went on the market for $22 million.

The prospect of gigantic homes along the ridgeline behind the Hollywood Sign dismayed local conservationists and government leaders such as L.A. City Councilman Tom LaBonge, who had been working to protect the land and add it to adjacent Griffith Park. Not only would development compromise the sign's pristine setting, but it would also cut off access for hikers, who had enjoyed the peak for years, and disrupt vital wildlife habitat. But the high selling price made the outlook for protection seem remote.

Then in April 2009, with real estate values plummeting, TPL managed to secure a one-year option to purchase Cahuenga Peak

for $12.5 million—just over half of the original listing price. And to focus attention on the need to raise this money, why not convert the Hollywood Sign into a campaign billboard?

In response, "the global and local community came together like you wouldn't believe," said actor Bill Pullman, one of several celebrities who joined TPL in the protection effort. "We had bake sales; we printed out flyers. Everyone in the neighborhood came together," a delighted Pullman later recalled. A Facebook page devoted to the campaign garnered nearly 27,000 fans, and donations small and large poured in. Major donors to the campaign included Hugh Hefner, the Tiffany Foundation, and local conservationist and philanthropist Aileen Getty.

After five days the wrapping came off, and the HOLLYWOOD letters—each 45 feet tall—reemerged one by one. But the effort launched by this singular messaging kept going strong, and in March 2012, supporters gathered near the sign to celebrate the dedication of Cahuenga Peak as protected open space. With LaBonge as emcee, Trust for Public Land staff unveiled the Aileen Getty Ridge Trail and the Hugh Hefner Overlook, both providing the public with new access to the chaparral-covered peak and its panoramic views of Los Angeles and the San Fernando Valley. Now Angeleños will forever have a place to get some perspective on fame and fortune.

Opposite top: Workers drape the Hollywood Sign to call attention to the Cahuenga Peak campaign. Signquest.com/The WallSticker. com. *Opposite bottom: A woman enjoys the views from Cahuenga Peak.* Rich Reid Photography.com. *Above: For several days the sign read "Save the Peak."* Rich Reid Photography.com.

"Urban opportunities require a different kind of spatial imagination. If there isn't a park, you have to find some-place that could be a park."

—Peter Harnik, director, TPL's Center for City Park Excellence

A three-mile-long elevated rail corridor will bring much-needed park space to Chicago's neighborhoods and become the city's next great park.

WHERE: Chicago, Illinois

YEARS: 2006–present

HIGHLIGHTS

- Chicago sets its sights on an elevated rail route that once serviced industries on the crowded Northwest Side.
- The Chicago Park District asks The Trust for Public Land to manage the private side of a public-private park project.
- TPL is raising funds and helping to create parks along the route, to provide trail access and more neighborhood park space.

SIDELIGHT

The Bloomingdale will cross 37 city streets on concrete viaducts.

Chicago's next great park will be nearly three miles long and 18 feet above street level. Since 2006, The Trust for Public Land has been working with the city, the Chicago Park District, and local supporters to create The Bloomingdale linear park and trail along a century-old rail corridor above Bloomingdale Avenue on the Northwest Side. Such creative reuse of elevated road- and railways can make space for a park where all the street-level real estate is spoken for. And whereas today the former rail line divides neighborhoods, the completed park will link communities while providing public open space and a path for walkers, runners, cyclists, and skaters.

Famed for its landmark lakeshore and downtown parks—including the award-winning Millennium Park, opened in 2004—Chicago is working to bring new parks and open space to the city's neighborhoods. The Bloomingdale will connect "four incredibly dense and diverse neighborhoods," Ben Helphand, president of the Friends of the Bloomingdale Trail, told *Land&People*

The Bloomingdale project will turn an elevated rail line through the heart of the city into a nearly three-mile-long park and trail. David Schalliol.

Left: A rendering of the future park and trail, slated to open end to end in 2014. Courtesy City of Chicago. Below: The Trust for Public Land is managing the private part of the public-private process and creating entry parks along the route, such as the new Albany Whipple Park. Brett Kramer Photography.

magazine in 2008. "The route goes by or near 12 different schools and a YMCA, and connects to the North Branch of the Chicago River and to the city's boulevard system and several other bike routes."

The Chicago Park District called on The Trust for Public Land to manage the private side of a public-private partnership assembled to carry out this ambitious project. Working closely with Friends of the Bloomingdale Trail, TPL has organized community meetings, worked to generate private support, and acquired parcels for new pocket parks that will provide trail access while creating additional park space in crowded neighborhoods.

Supporter-in-chief of The Bloomingdale is Mayor Rahm Emanuel, who has made its completion a priority for his first term. Design and engineering work is under way along with community meetings to guide design of the access parks. The elevated trail will be open and accessible from end to end in the fall of 2014, with additional enhancements completed in 2015.

"The Bloomingdale is our most visionary open space project, with the power to transform the city and tell a story about its people."

—Rahm Emanuel, mayor of Chicago

CHATTANOOGA GREENWAYS

"We made a conscious effort to pitch our quality of life, including all we've done to revitalize downtown, create parks and green space, clean up our air, and generally be good stewards of the environment."

—Trevor Hamilton, vice president for economic development, Chattanooga Area Chamber of Commerce

A Rust Belt city reinvents itself and revives its economy with a regional network of greenways and trails that connect people with cherished natural and cultural resources.

WHERE: Chattanooga, Tennessee

YEARS: 1994–present

HIGHLIGHTS
- The Trust for Public Land works with the city of Chattanooga and Hamilton County on land acquisition, planning, and funding for the regional greenway system.
- Chattanooga's Greenway Master Plan is creating greenways along tributaries of the Tennessee River, linked to the popular downtown Riverpark.
- TPL helps raise $2.5 million to preserve 92 acres on Stringer's Ridge, the city's green backdrop.

SIDELIGHT
Nearly a half-mile long, the Walnut Street Bridge on Chattanooga's Riverpark is one of the longest pedestrian bridges in the world.

WHAT'S NEXT?
TPL will help extend the Riverpark to Moccasin Bend and expand tributary greenways.

Like so many waterfront cities, Chattanooga long saw its river as a resource for commerce, not for people. But when the Rust Belt went bust, the city's leaders set out to map a future based on quality of life, with the Tennessee River at its center. They built new attractions along the riverfront, including a world-class aquarium, and began work on the ten-mile Riverpark

"The vision of the greenway
was an attempt to get people
to see their city with completely
new eyes—to believe that
Chattanooga, with our
mountains and ridges, our
river, creeks, and valleys,
was as beautiful as Portland
or San Francisco."

—Rick Montague, former leader
of the public forum
Chattanooga Venture

greenway, which has become the spine of a trail system reaching up tributary streams into the neighborhoods. The new waterfront amenities and easy access to open space have attracted new business, including a Volkswagen manufacturing plant. On the evening news in 1969, Walter Cronkite pronounced Chattanooga "the dirtiest city in America"; today it is envied for its thriving economy founded on a healthy river, a revitalized downtown, and plenty of green space.

The Trust for Public Land began working in Chattanooga in 1994 and in the years since has become a crucial partner in building the greenway system and protecting green spaces of historic importance—notably by helping to add Chattanooga's civil war battlefields to the Chickamauga and Chattanooga National Military Park. Today TPL is helping to double the length of the Riverpark and build tributary greenways by acquiring land and easements. In one recent project, TPL organized a fundraising effort to create a city park on Stringer's Ridge, an iconic open space overlooking downtown, and is currently working to build eight miles of trails there.

Chattanooga's bold gamble to base its future on open space and riverfront access has clearly paid off. "Companies want their employees to have places to walk and bike and enjoy the land," David Crockett, director of the city's Office of Sustainability, told TPL's *Land&People* magazine in 2011. By investing in riverfront parks, greenways, and trails, Chattanooga has positioned itself for success. America's one-time "dirtiest city" is now showing other cities how to thrive: by reconnecting people with the land.

FLORIDA RAIL TRAILS

The Trust for Public Land helps Florida build one of the nation's largest networks of trails on former rail corridors.

WHERE: Florida

YEARS: 2005–present

HIGHLIGHTS

- In recent years, Florida communities have created hundreds of miles of rail trails, many with TPL's help.
- Rail trails have contributed hugely to the economy of the communities they traverse and to the health of users.
- To date, TPL has facilitated rail-to-trail projects in St. Petersburg, Leesburg, Tallahassee, Gainesville, Sarasota, and Orlando.

SIDELIGHT

A rail corridor acquired by TPL for Sarasota once carried circus trains to the Ringling Bros. winter quarters.

WHAT'S NEXT?

Planned trails would carry cyclists 300 miles northward from St. Petersburg and link St. Augustine, Orlando, and the Kennedy Space Center in a 500-mile loop.

With its benign climate, level topography, and abundant rail corridors that once carried goods and tourists through the Sunshine State, Florida has become a hotbed of the rails-to-trails movement. On routes such as the Fred Marquis Pinellas Trail—one of the nation's best-used rail trails, stretching 37 miles from St. Petersburg north to Tarpon Springs—cyclists of all stripes are joined by walkers, runners, in-line skaters, strolling seniors, dog exercisers, and moms pushing baby buggies. Trail users improve their health and fitness, bike commuters save on gas, and communities touched by the trails thrive.

By working with the state, communities, and railroad companies, The Trust for Public Land has helped create or expand many of Florida's rail trails. It helped connect the Pinellas Trail directly to downtown St. Petersburg via a two-mile extension. Just to the south, it acquired for Sarasota County a 13-mile segment of a route that once carried circus trains to the winter home of the Ringling Bros. and Barnum & Bailey circus. In 2010, TPL added nine miles of protected trail corridor to the Nature Coast State Trail, which traverses rural northwest Florida near Gainesville and Tallahassee. The Dinky Line Trail—so named for the narrow-gauge tracks of

the Orlando and Winter Park Railway—was built on TPL-acquired land and now is part of Orlando's popular Urban Trail network. Since 2005, The Trust for Public Land has completed rail-trail projects in a half-dozen Florida communities, with more on the way.

Above: A new rail trail connects downtown St. Petersburg to the 37-mile Pinellas Trail. Darcy Kiefel. *Below: Riders enjoy the Legacy Trail, which runs from Sarasota to Venice.* Darcy Kiefel.

"The trail has become the mother tree of our town. Everything has branched out from it."

—Bob Ironsmith, community development director, Dunedin, Florida, on the Pinellas Trail

SANTA FE RAILYARD PARK + PLAZA

"It's the largest park TPL has ever built, involving dozens of TPL employees and a thousand volunteers."

—Jenny Parks,
former TPL New Mexico
state director

"No private developer in his right mind would have done this, ever."

—Steve Robinson,
architect

Right: TPL acquired the land for the park and plaza and later oversaw its design. William Poole. Below: A water tank reminiscent of the days of steam locomotives is a central feature of the park's irrigation system. Don J. Usner.

A former railyard becomes a 12-acre park and plaza celebrating a city's history, creativity, and diversity.

WHERE: Santa Fe, New Mexico

YEARS: 1995–2008

HIGHLIGHTS

- The Trust for Public Land acquires a 50-acre downtown railyard for Santa Fe.
- At the city's request, TPL raises funds for and oversees development of the park and plaza.
- The park includes a farmers' market, railyard-style water tower, native garden, and landscaped play area.

SIDELIGHT

The Acequia Madre—a seven-mile irrigation ditch dating from the Spanish settlement era—crosses the property. Also on the property: a colony of prairie dogs that were relocated to a national wildlife refuge.

Santa Fe, with its historic central plaza, is well known as a tourist mecca. But when you enter the city's newest downtown park, it feels local. Arising on a site where trains once deposited visitors from all over the country, the Railyard Park + Plaza embodies many dimensions of this special community: its history, native landscape, and diverse cultures. Residents (tourists too!) browse through a farmers' market, one of the nation's top ten in attendance. They stroll or bike on pathways that trace the rail tracks and wind into adjacent neighborhoods, or along the banks of a 400-year-old *acequia* that once irrigated farm fields. They work plots in a community garden, one of them based on a Native American model, or gather on mild evenings for outdoor movie screenings. Kids scamper around an elaborate circular play area that evokes Southwestern cliff dwellings. And commuters arrive and depart on a new train linking Santa Fe with towns to the south.

The people of Santa Fe had to wait decades for their downtown park, but it was worth the wait. In the beginning they had a treasure in the rough: 50 acres in the heart of the city, preserved from development since the 1880s by the sprawling railroad complex but by the early 1990s a collection of derelict buildings, old tracks, and dusty lots. So when the railyard's owner proposed a dense six-story development, city leaders determined to buy the land instead—at least in part for a community park and gathering place. At the city's request, The Trust for Public Land in 1995 acquired the railyard at millions less than its appraised value. The transaction reserved 12 acres for a public park and plaza.

In 2001, the city asked The Trust for Public Land to extend its work on the project by overseeing fundraising for the new park and plaza, as well as planning, design, and construction.

TPL helped raise an eventual $13.7 million and coordinated an extensive community planning effort, during which some 6,000 residents voiced their ideas for what should happen to the former railyard. "Residents are the experts, and we needed to learn from them," Steve Robinson, a local architect who worked on the community planning effort, told *Land&People* magazine in 2009. Equipped with this knowledge, TPL launched an international design competition, chose the team that would execute the master plan, oversaw the seven-year construction process, and, once the park was opened, helped form a new Railyard Park Stewards group to care for the park and develop programs.

The park's grand opening in September 2008 drew 20,000 people representing all of Santa Fe. "I had never before seen such a true cross-section of the community," said Carmella Padilla, who grew up here and worked on the project as both a volunteer and a TPL consultant. Since then, the park has fulfilled its promise of becoming the heart of community life in Santa Fe, hosting school and charity events, concerts, arts and crafts markets, the annual fiesta, and the city's 400th anniversary observation.

TPL staffer Smitty Smith and his daughter, Greta, explore an acequia *(irrigation ditch) from the Spanish settlement era that was restored for the new park.* Don J. Usner.

"The park has lifted up the people along with many of the properties surrounding it."

—Bertha Martin,
founding member,
the Mildred Helms Park
Resurrection Committee

The Trust for Public Land works with the city, foundations, community members, and schoolchildren to bring new parks and playgrounds to neighborhoods most in need.

WHERE: Newark, New Jersey

YEARS: 1976–present

HIGHLIGHTS
- Since 1995, TPL has helped create 10 new parks and playgrounds and marshaled more than $30 million in public and philanthropic funds.
- The new Nat Turner Park is Newark's largest city-owned park, providing recreation for 19,000 residents.
- As a lead partner in the Newark Riverfront Park, TPL is helping the city reclaim its Passaic River waterfront.

SIDELIGHT
In 2010, the Mount Vernon Elementary School playground was recognized for design excellence by the New Jersey Recreation and Park Association.

WHAT'S NEXT?
Finishing the Newark Riverfront Park, completing final phases of Jesse Allen Park, and strategizing with the city and school district on future projects.

Top: Sister Mary Dwyer and students at St. Columba Peace Playground, 1995. Steven Tucker. Right: Hanging out at the new Quitman Street Community School playground, 2007. John Rae.

In 2008, a new playground opened at the Mount Vernon Elementary School in Newark's Vailsburg neighborhood. Though the playground was relatively small, its opening was national news because of a high-profile tragedy that had occurred at the spot one year earlier, when four local college students were brutally attacked and three murdered there. Thanks to determined neighbors, their equally determined mayor, and generous donors, The Trust for Public Land was able to work with the school and the community to convert a nearly bare asphalt schoolyard scarred by violence into an award-winning, state-of-the-art playspace. It was to be, in the words of TPL's Newark director, Scott Dvorak, "a safe place where new memories can be made."

That phrase might well summarize the goal of much of TPL's 30-plus years of work in Newark—a city where less than half of all kids live within walking distance of a park or playground. Newark was the site of TPL's first projects outside California, in 1976. Today, thanks to a continuing partnership with the city under Mayor Cory Booker and the generous support of local

Mayor Cory Booker, a staunch supporter of parks and playgrounds, cuts the ribbon to open Nat Turner Park in 2009. TPL helped turn a blighted lot into Newark's largest city-owned park. J. Avery Wham Photography.

"We believe that parks, playgrounds, and new public open spaces can play a vital role in sustaining livable neighborhoods and building the city's economic future."

—Cory A. Booker, mayor of Newark

foundations, TPL is still at work there, helping to create neighborhood parks and playgrounds, including a seven-acre park on the long-neglected banks of the Passaic River.

TPL ramped up its work in Newark in the 1990s as part of its Green Cities Initiative, with a focus on rehabilitating schoolyards and building parks in park-poor communities. In 1995, TPL worked with Sister Mary Dwyer, then principal of St. Columba School in the East Ward ("a beat-up neighborhood where day-to-day life is a struggle," Dwyer called it) to create a playground for her 350 students. TPL negotiated for the purchase of six separate lots totaling about an acre, secured funding, and oversaw design and construction. "Every day the children asked when the playground would be ready," Sister Mary told *Land&People* in 1996. "You could see the joy on their faces when they were finally allowed to enter."

Since then, TPL has completed or rebuilt ten Newark parks or playgrounds, including one at McKinley Elementary School, where students worked with design professionals to transform a parking lot; Mildred Helms Park, on a three-acre city-owned site next to the Clinton Avenue Early Childhood Development Center; and Nat Turner Park, which rose from a blighted nine-acre lot to become Newark's largest city-owned park, providing recreation for a neighborhood of 19,000, including 7,000 children. When the first phase of eight-acre Jesse Allen Park opened in 2009—two more phases are under way—it featured the city's first skateboard park.

As important as parks are for the neighborhoods, Mayor Booker and others see them as key to Newark's broader renaissance. The Newark Riverfront Park is intended to generate the kind of social and economic revitalization that the recovery of riverfronts has worked in other industrial cities. With a design developed through public meetings, the park on the Passaic will include walking and biking trails, a dock for boating access, a riverfront boardwalk, a river overlook with an osprey rook, and native plantings.

CITY PARK, NEW ORLEANS

"New Orleans is rightly proud of its large, centrally located City Park and Audubon Park, but it doesn't have many smaller parks in neighborhoods. This is a chance to build a park system that links the city together."

—Larry Schmidt, director, TPL's New Orleans office

Right: TPL raised funds and oversaw the restoration of Big Lake after Hurricane Katrina. Larry Schmidt. *Below: City Park offers amusements, including a miniature train ride.* Chris Granger.

Restoring historic City Park and building new parks helps New Orleans recover from disaster.

WHERE: New Orleans, Louisiana

YEARS: 2005–present

HIGHLIGHTS
- When Hurricane Katrina lays waste to 1,300-acre City Park, New Orleanians and outsiders contribute labor and funds to rebuild it.
- The Trust for Public Land targets 50 acres near the park entrance for a $2.5 million campaign to restore and enhance Big Lake and add needed amenities.
- New Orleans makes new parks and greenways central to its master plan for a renewed city, with TPL as a key partner.

SIDELIGHT
After the hurricane, thousands of volunteers helped restore City Park, including a volunteer grass-mowing and clean-up crew self-named the "Mow-rons."

WHAT'S NEXT?
Supporting the development of the 3.1-mile Lafitte Greenway and adding new parks in the neighborhoods

When Hurricane Katrina tore through New Orleans in August 2005, it left 90 percent of historic City Park—an area as large as New York's Central Park—underwater and park infrastructure in shambles. Since 1854, City Park has been the city's outdoor heart and soul. Before the disaster, more than 11 million people visited each year to play sports, stroll among the majestic live oaks, tour the New Orleans Museum of Art, or attend weddings and other celebrations.

Work to rebuild City Park got started as soon as the floodwaters receded, as volunteers descended on the park to clear trash, mow lawns, and restore courts and play areas. "People were anxious to get back in the park," City Park CEO Bob Becker told *Land&People* magazine in 2007, "and they were willing to help get it going."

Hoping to do its part, The Trust for Public Land focused on 50 acres near the park entrance and the museum, including Big Lake and an abandoned golf course. Following a $2.5 million fundraising drive, TPL oversaw the conversion of the golf course into a meadow, reshaped the topography for better access to the lake, added a pedestrian-and-bike path, and constructed a boat dock, bringing beloved but long-absent paddleboats back to City Park. Opened in 2009, the new Big Lake Trail and meadow today welcomes over 150,000 visitors annually.

The restoration was only part of a broader effort by TPL to build parks for the new New Orleans, where civic leaders are re-thinking the role of parks and open space after Katrina. In partnership with the city, TPL is using its GIS mapping technology to map where newly vacant land could be protected for parks, playgrounds, water retention, trails, sports fields, or community farms and gardens. Already under way: the redesign of Mickey Markey Park in the historic Ninth Ward/Bywater neighborhood and acquisition of 18 acres for the 3.1-mile Lafitte Greenway—

the city's first new park in two decades. Ultimately the greenway will extend from the French Quarter through Treme and Mid-City to Lakeview, near Lake Pontchartrain—linking parks, trails, public spaces, and playgrounds.

No American city is more in need of the physical and psycho-logical benefits of parks than still-recovering New Orleans, and City Park's slow rise from the ruins has been an important symbol. From the restoration of City Park to the greening of neighborhoods, parks are proving key to a full recovery.

TPL's work in City Park following Hurricane Katrina kicked off a series of projects to help create parks and green spaces in a dramatically changed New Orleans. Chris Granger.

Above: A father and daughter show off radishes from a garden on the Visitacion Valley Greenway. Rich Reid Photography. com. Right: Grace Marchant in her garden along the Filbert Steps, protected in 1986. L. Habegger.

"Our partnership with TPL helps families thrive by rebuilding dilapidated parks and playgrounds in neighborhoods that need them most."

—Philip Ginsburg, general manager, San Francisco Recreation and Parks

The Trust for Public Land partners with government, donors, and diverse communities to create parks and conserve open space across its home city.

WHERE: San Francisco, California

YEARS: 1973–present

HIGHLIGHTS

- TPL develops its community-centric design process, ensuring that parks reflect neighborhood character and needs.
- Vacant lots in park-poor Visitacion Valley are transformed into a greenway with a plaza, a community garden, a playground, and a native plant garden.
- With lead funding from major local donors, TPL refurbishes three much-needed neighborhood parks and playgrounds.

SIDELIGHT

The new energy-efficient clubhouse at the renovated Hayes Valley playground is insulated with shredded and recycled denim jeans.

WHAT'S NEXT?

Construction on the refurbished Boeddeker Park is slated for completion in late 2013.

Within San Francisco's few dozen square miles, the spirit of innovation seems concentrated. Ample evidence includes the birth here of The Trust for Public Land—a new kind of land-saving organization—and the creative array of parks TPL has helped build in its home city. The first came way back in 1973, when the family of Daniel Koshland decided to endow a new park in a core neighborhood that desperately needed one. (See story on page 33.) One of the latest, Hayes Valley Playground, is just blocks away in the same neighborhood—a vivid new space that replaced a dilapidated old playground. Renovated in partnership with the city and the support of TPL donors, the new park features sparkling mosaics, modern play structures, raised garden beds, and a high-tech "green" clubhouse.

Hayes Valley Playground is one of three parks being refurbished by TPL in collaboration with five major local donors—Banana Republic, Levi Strauss Foundation, McKesson, Pacific Gas and Electric Company, and Wells Fargo; each contributed $1 million to kick-start the fundraising. "In today's difficult budget climate, San Francisco's recreation and park department can't do it alone," said the department's general manager, Philip Ginsburg, about the successful partnership. TPL is leading the planning, design, and construction.

Another San Francisco trademark is community involvement, and the first step in these park upgrades was an extensive neighborhood planning process, the kind TPL has been managing since its earliest days. Through public meetings, design workshops, and ongoing discussion with community groups, neighborhood needs are identified and addressed in the design. At Hayes Valley it was play areas for small children and fitness

equipment for adults, among other things. At another of the three target parks, Boeddeker Park in the city's Tenderloin district, the key goal was to create a safe, welcoming space in a low-income, dangerous neighborhood. Long known as the "prison park" because of its forbidding fence, the park soon will feature a more open design with benches, walking paths, patios for tai chi practice, and many green components. The third site, Balboa Park, sprawls over 25 acres in outlying neighborhoods and attracts visitors from across the city for sports and group activities. Here residents most wanted improvements to serve the surrounding community, such as upgraded playgrounds—to give a citywide park a local identity.

Over 40 years, TPL has helped create or renew 18 parks in San Francisco, as diverse as the city's neighborhoods. On picturesque Telegraph Hill, TPL was instrumental in preserving a dramatic strip of green and flowers along the steep Filbert Steps overlooking the bay. TPL originally protected the Grace Marchant Garden—named for a local resident who long maintained it—in 1986 with

the help of a public "buy-a-square-inch" campaign. Twenty years later, when another small portion of the garden was at risk, TPL preserved that as well.

On Potrero Hill, where gentrified blocks bump up against public housing projects, TPL oversaw fundraising for another playground, then its planning and renovation. During the community planning phase, residents from both segments of the neighborhood stipulated that the renovated play space should foster inclusiveness and celebrate the diversity of Potrero Hill.

And in Visitacion Valley, a working-class district southeast of downtown, TPL worked for a decade with neighborhood groups to transform a strip of weedy, garbage-strewn lots—an unused utility right-of-way—into an expansive hillside greenway that brings nature close to home for thousands of residents. Creating the greenway also gave residents a sense of empowerment—that they could work together to make things better. As neighborhood leader Fran Martin said in 2004, "The greenway is like a seed, and we hope it will sprout through the community."

> "I hope our work shows this neighborhood that it's valued. The residents deserve a park that's inviting and attractive to users of all ages."
>
> —Philip Vitale,
> TPL project manager
> for Balboa Park

The refurbishing of Potrero Hill Playground in 2007 is one of a series of projects with the city that continue to this day. Over 40 years, TPL has helped create or renew 18 San Francisco parks. Nita Winter Photography.

ATLANTA BELTLINE

"Nowhere in the United States does another city have Atlanta's opportunity to reinvent itself in such a dramatic fashion."

—Alexander Garvin, author, *The BeltLine Emerald Necklace: Atlanta's New Public Realm*

A city seizes a rare chance to create a dramatic system of parks, mixed-use developments, and transit for the 21st century.

WHERE: Atlanta, Georgia

YEARS: 2005–present

HIGHLIGHTS

- The BeltLine will encircle downtown along 22 miles of former rail corridor, linking 47 neighborhoods and creating or improving 8 parks.
- A Trust for Public Land–commissioned report generates vital momentum.
- TPL acquires 33 parcels to date—totaling 83 acres, saving the city millions, and ensuring the land's future.

SIDELIGHT
The new lake at the Historic Fourth Ward Park is filled with stormwater, preventing local flooding without expensive underground piping.

As Trust for Public Land President Will Rogers has said, "Our greatest skill may be to recognize powerful new ideas and throw our weight behind them." Just such an idea was floated in 1999 by Georgia Tech graduate student Ryan Gravel, who saw that Atlanta's heritage as a railroad hub could help the traffic-clogged city chart its transportation future. Gravel's master's thesis proposed a transit loop along the abandoned rail corridors that encircled downtown. TPL got wind of it, saw that parks should be a key part of the plan, and in 2004 commissioned urban planner Alex Garvin to assess the landscape and produce a report that would help Atlantans visualize what a BeltLine system of parks, trails, and transit might look like.

By describing the proposed BeltLine as Atlanta's "Emerald Necklace," Garvin positioned the project in the great tradition of 19th-century park visionaries like Frederick Olmsted (whose original "emerald necklace" decorates Boston). It's the most

In addition to being beautiful, the lake and water features at Historic Fourth Ward Park retain stormwater in a neighborhood once plagued by flooding. Darcy Kiefel.

ambitious vision for a connected system of parks and transit any U.S. city has committed to: bringing into public ownership more than 1,000 acres along a 22-mile loop of historic railroad, connecting 47 neighborhoods via trails and green spaces, creating or expanding eight parks, and truly transforming the city.

Enthusiasm spread fast. Even before the effort was truly organized, TPL began acquiring properties along the BeltLine for new parks and to date has helped add more than 83 acres of parkland along the BeltLine loop, including Atlanta's first skatepark. Today TPL works in concert with the Atlanta BeltLine, Inc.—appointed by the Atlanta Development Authority—and the Atlanta BeltLine Partnership, a nonprofit that raises private funds for the BeltLine.

Among the key goals of the project are to promote park equity by building parks in neighborhoods that lack them and to spark economic development.

Already the BeltLine is being hailed as a pioneering park effort of the 21st century—a national model in how it links park-making with new transit, economic development, and community revitalization. But getting this far took huge leaps of faith and for residents across Atlanta to realize that the project will be good for both business and neighborhoods. As Jim Langford, formerly TPL's Georgia state director, told *Land&People* magazine, "Everyone involved with the BeltLine was motivated by the power of the idea."

When completed, the Atlanta BeltLine will provide parks, trails, and public transit along a 22-mile former rail corridor encircling downtown. Darcy Kiefel.

"These investments are not only helping to redefine accessible public space in the city, but The Trust for Public Land's innovative approach to participatory design is reshaping how our children engage with their neighborhoods and schools."

—David Bragdon, director, Mayor's Office of Long-Term Planning and Sustainability, New York City

Above: An asphalt school lot becomes a playground at P.S. 180 in Harlem, 2006. Before: Mary Alice Lee. *After:* J. Avery Wham Photography. *Below: Enjoying the new playground at P.S. 242, which also serves the Future Leaders Institute charter school.* Yola Monakhov.

The Trust for Public Land helps create more than 120 neighborhood playgrounds and parks by transforming asphalt schoolyards in park-poor communities around the city.

WHERE: New York, New York

YEARS: 1996–present

HIGHLIGHTS

- Looking for places to create neighborhood open space, TPL identifies schoolyards as an overlooked resource and begins the program with donated funds.
- Beginning in 2004, partnerships with New York City's Department of Education and Mayor Bloomberg's PlaNYC expand the program.
- Success depends on participatory design and partnership with a community group to foster stewardship.

SIDELIGHT

Playground features added at the request of student designers include a dedicated hair-braiding area at P.S. 242 in Harlem.

WHAT'S NEXT?

With funding from the city's Department of Environmental Protection, building natural "green infrastructure" elements into ten new playgrounds to capture stormwater before it can pollute the city's waterways.

In April 2011, the students of P.S. 181 in Brooklyn's East Flatbush neighborhood celebrated the new community playground they helped design and couldn't wait to start using. "It turned out to be exactly what we wanted," eighth-grader Peter Bonner told the *New York Daily News*. Forty students had been meeting for half the school year, at lunchtime and after class, with landscape designers and staff from The Trust for Public Land, to discuss what would go into their playground. Some wanted a stage for student plays and music, so a 30-seat amphitheater was added to the one-acre layout. Others wanted a jungle gym, or an open field where kids could play football without getting scraped up on concrete. They got both. Children and designers used paper models to create a scale design for the space. "All the students involved made great contributions," said Principal Lowell Coleman, "and it gives them a great sense of pride."

Turning a barren asphalt schoolyard into a real playground and community park requires many steps: planning, participatory design, construction, and partnering with community groups to guarantee ongoing stewardship. To date, with support from its donors, TPL has managed this entire process to rebuild more than 50 New York City public school playgrounds—and supervised participatory design on dozens of others for a total of more than 120 playgrounds citywide. The goal is not only to serve schoolchildren—1,200 of them in the case of P.S. 181—but also to provide much-needed recreational open space for the surrounding neighborhood. P.S. 181 follows the pattern for these projects: it has an enthusiastic, committed principal and an established neighborhood group to help care for the playground, keep it open after school hours, and devise programming.

These ingredients for what makes a neighborhood park or playground work were discovered over many years of experience in New York. Starting in 1996, building on its work of supporting community gardens, TPL began working to create more recreational space in neighborhoods. But vacant land was in short supply. "We felt that schoolyards were really an underutilized asset," says Mary Alice Lee, director of TPL's NYC Playground Program. Early projects were accomplished mainly with private funding from generous foundations and donors, but soon the city began to take notice, especially as making playgrounds dovetailed with its rising emphasis on student health and fitness.

In 2004, Mayor Michael Bloomberg's office announced a partnership between TPL and the city's Department of Education to build 25 new playgrounds in public schoolyards over the next five years. That pilot project brought vital, community-planned playgrounds to schools like C.S. 66 in the South Bronx, P.S. 189 in Harlem, and J.H.S. 216 in Queens. And thanks to the city's buy-in, every dollar raised by The Trust for Public Land was augmented by $2 from the Department of Education. A few years later, TPL and the city expanded their partnership as part of Mayor Bloomberg's PlaNYC 2030, an ambitious initiative to bring parks and recreation space within easy reach of all of New York's children.

Like all of TPL's work in New York—whether protecting community gardens or revitalizing neglected waterfronts—success in creating well-used playgrounds is based on the land-and-people principle. Says Andy Stone, director of the NYC Parks for People program, "What makes the land valuable is the people's ongoing engagement with it, constantly reinvigorating its purpose." Of all the lessons learned over a decade and half, the community engagement imperative—from planning through stewardship—is paramount. It's what makes a place special. As seventh-grader Chelsea McFarlane of P.S. 66 said about her new playground, "Everything about the place is special. It's the best park in the neighborhood."

"Inner-city children don't know about employment opportunities besides professional athletics, rap music, and entertainment.... Maybe just one student will get it into his or her head that they could become a landscape architect."

—Stephen Walton, fifth-grade teacher, C.S. 66, South Bronx

Students at P.S. 38 in Brooklyn plan their new playground and community park. Alan Chin.

"Parks in my district are our backyards—where we congregate, play, and exercise."

—Gloria Molina,
Los Angeles County supervisor,
East L.A.

"For local residents who don't have easy access to the beach or the mountains, for those who don't get a break from the concrete and asphalt, the Cornfield will be a treasure, a refuge, a field of dreams."

—Richard Polanco,
former California state senator

Above: The Fitness Zone at Ruben F. Salazar Park is one of nearly 30 TPL has installed in greater Los Angeles. Rich Reid Photography.com. *Right: Creating access to the Los Angeles River has been a focus of TPL's work.* Rich Reid Photography.com.

The Trust for Public Land is helping to connect people with nature and create recreational open space in some of the nation's most park-poor communities.

WHERE: Los Angeles, California

YEARS: 1996–present

HIGHLIGHTS
• TPL helps create parks along the Los Angeles River and the first state park in Los Angeles, near crowded Chinatown.
• An ongoing commitment to densely settled Maywood yields two parks, with a third on the drawing board.
• Trust for Public Land Fitness Zones in 29 parks help thousands of Angeleños get—and stay—fit.

SIDELIGHT
The city of Maywood began in 1919 as a development named for May Wood, a popular employee of the development company.

When The Trust for Public Land protected Cahuenga Peak in the center of sprawling Los Angeles, in 2010, it was the first many residents had heard of the organization. (See page 84.) In fact, TPL had been working in and around Los Angeles since it acquired Bee Canyon for what is now O'Melveny Park, one of its very first projects in 1973. In the years since, TPL has conserved more than 10,000 acres including the Ballona Wetlands in Playa del Rey, launched a multimillion-dollar park-building program in low-income neighborhoods, and installed 41 Fitness Zones in existing public parks.

Despite California's reputation as an outdoor paradise, Los Angeles residents are often isolated from public parks and green space. In fact, less than a third of children in Los Angeles County live within walking distance of a park or playground—a stat TPL has been working to change.

TPL's longest-running project in L.A. has been helping the city realize its vision for parks and open space along the Los Angeles River—long tamed with concrete to control flooding and one of the city's most underused open space resources. Since the 1980s dedicated advocates have been working to create a 51-mile greenway from the river's mountain headwaters to the Pacific Ocean. With other nonprofits and public agencies, TPL has worked to string together existing parks and create new ones. Current projects along the river include the Aliso Creek Confluence Park in Reseda, which will include native plants, a pedestrian bridge, and a stretch of the Los Angeles River Bike Path, and a new park at the former Will J. Reid Boy Scout property in Long Beach.

One highlight of this work came in 2001, when TPL acquired and cleaned up a 32-acre railyard near the river to create the Los Angeles State Historic Park, the first state park in the city. The site, known as the "Cornfields" for the crop grown there in former times, is on the edge of Chinatown, and the new park has brought welcome open space to that crowded and park-poor neighborhood.

Downriver, in the city of Maywood, TPL acquired and cleaned up seven adjoining industrial parcels—an EPA superfund site— for the Maywood Riverfront Park, completed in 2006. The most densely populated city west of the Mississippi, Maywood is desperately in need of park space, and TPL has stayed engaged there—supervising the design and construction of the Pine Avenue Pocket Park in 2011 and now working to create a new park on Maywood Avenue.

Elsewhere in L.A., TPL is helping neighbors in Watts transform a vacant lot into Monitor Avenue Park so that kids have a safe place to play. The Patton Street Pocket Park and Community Garden will serve residents of Echo Park, a dense neighborhood on the edge of downtown. Fundraising is nearing completion for Larch Avenue Park in Lawndale and the half-acre Madison Avenue Park in East Hollywood, which will feature a dynamic new playground and community garden.

Seven of nine planned new parks will include Fitness Zones, outdoor gyms equipped with tough, all-weather exercise equipment that provide a place to work out for people who mostly can't afford health-club fees.

TPL acquired and cleaned up an EPA superfund site to create the Maywood Riverfront Park, opened in 2006. One additional park has been created and another is planned for this densely settled city. Rich Reid Photography.com.

NATURAL LANDS

THE AMERICAN CONSERVATION MOVEMENT was born of the impulse to preserve our nation's wildest places. Natural lands serve as essential habitat for wildlife and plants, safeguard water and other natural resources, and help mitigate the effects of climate change. They also serve as America's outdoor playgrounds and places of inspiration, offering irreplaceable contact with wild nature. Beginning with its earliest natural lands projects in California, Idaho, and Florida, The Trust for Public Land has employed its evolving financial, legal, and real estate expertise to bring threatened natural and wild lands into public ownership in 46 of the 50 states and in the U.S. Virgin Islands and Puerto Rico, helping conservation leaders balance the demands of growth with the need to protect wilderness and open space.

A hiker in Gates Pass, near Tucson, Arizona, protected in 1998. Nevada Wier.

THE COLUMBIA RIVER GORGE

"This gorge is special to us because it contains such a unique variety of all the things that are important to us: natural beauty, cultural heritage, the blending of people with the landscape."

—Lauri Aunan,
former executive director,
Friends of the Columbia Gorge

Right: Children play in Rowena Dell, protected in a series of projects in the early 1990s. George Wuerthner. *Below: Windsurfers near Hood River, Oregon.* Ron Cronin.

The Trust for Public Land helps protect an iconic natural feature of the Pacific Northwest as a National Scenic Area.

WHERE: Oregon and Washington

YEARS: 1979–present

HIGHLIGHTS
- In 1986, at the urging of TPL and the Friends of the Columbia Gorge and with the support of former senator Mark Hatfield, Congress authorizes the Columbia Gorge National Scenic Area.
- Over 26 years, TPL protects 17,000 acres in the Columbia Gorge in more than 80 transactions.
- Conserved lands include the Cape Horn overlook and the Dalles Ranch at the gorge's eastern end.

SIDELIGHT
In 2008, TPL was able to negotiate the purchase of the only house ever built on Cape Horn—a structure later demolished to permanently protect the scenic overlook.

WHAT'S NEXT?
TPL continues to work with partners to protect scenic and vulnerable landscapes in the gorge.

The Columbia River Gorge has long been a favorite outdoor destination for residents of the Pacific Northwest. The 85 miles of the river before it reaches Portland, Oregon, flows through dramatic and diverse terrain. The gorge is home to large and small communities, agriculture, industry, railways, major dams, and an interstate highway; but also to national forests, state parks, tumbling waterfalls, sheer basalt cliffs, and wildflower-carpeted hillsides. Since 1970s, farsighted and determined conservationists have been working to protect the gorge's natural landscapes for their recreational and scenic value. The Trust for Public Land has been there since the beginning, partnering with generous donors, federal agencies, and the states of Oregon and Washington on more than 80 projects to date, protecting more than 17,000 acres.

Those projects range from the western end of the gorge, where TPL helped safeguard the spectacular overlooks at Cape Horn and Mt. Pleasant, to the Dalles Mountain Ranch, more than 6,000 acres at the eastern gateway. At Lyle Point, by the junction of the Columbia and Klickitat Rivers, TPL fended off a subdivision slated to be built on sacred burial sites of the Yakama Nation—one of several tribes that have lived and fished for salmon on the river's banks for millennia—later conveying the land to the Yakama. And in 2002, TPL helped protect the estuary where the Hood River spills its glacier-fed waters into the Columbia, to the benefit of salmon, schoolchildren who study their habitat, and windsurfers who relish the stiff winds that sweep this mighty confluence.

With so much land under so many jurisdictions, it was clear that the gorge needed some kind of comprehensive federal oversight to ensure coherent protection. In November 1986, that goal finally was realized with the creation of the Columbia Gorge National Scenic Area—the crowning achievement of longtime TPL donor and partner Nancy Russell, who founded the Friends of the Columbia Gorge, and former Oregon senator Mark Hatfield, who guided the act through Congress. A new kind of federally protected area where public and private lands mingle, the scenic area is managed in partnership by the bordering counties and states, the U.S. Forest Service, affected Native American tribes, and a 13-member commission, to represent the region's myriad stakeholders. More than 292,000 acres are regulated by the legislation, which prohibits development in certain areas, discourages sprawl, and promotes protection of scenic properties.

Bowen Blair, who was executive director of Friends of the Columbia Gorge and later directed TPL's Oregon office, believes that TPL's work in the gorge demonstrates what can be achieved by an organization with a vision for an entire region. "By building public support, by bringing in private money, by being willing to take on controversial projects that no public agency would risk, we were able to show people what could be done," he told *Land&People* in 1996. As a result, one of the nation's premier natural and recreation spaces will be forever accessible to residents of fast-growing Portland, and Vancouver, Washington, across the river—along with people living up and down the gorge and countless visitors to the Northwest.

Looking northwest up the Columbia Gorge past Crown Point State Park. Since the mid-1980s, TPL has completed more than 80 projects protecting more than 17,000 acres in the gorge. Gary Weathers/Tetra Images/Corbis.

THE NORTHWOODS

Above: The gift of the Forest Lodge property to the U.S. Forest Service led to the creation of TPL's Northwoods Land Protection Fund. Elizabeth Bouchard/ USFS. Right: Conservationist Sigurd Olson at his writing cabin at Listening Point. Don Albrecht/Northland College.

"Wilderness to the people of America is a spiritual necessity, an antidote to the high pressure of modern life, a means of regaining serenity and equilibrium."

—Sigurd F. Olson

The Trust for Public Land works to protect the iconic land-scapes of the Midwest's Northwoods and preserve a heritage that is at risk.

WHERE: Northern Minnesota, Wisconsin, and Michigan

YEARS: 1980s–present

HIGHLIGHTS
- Building on work here since the 1980s, TPL launches its Northwoods Initiative to protect land throughout the region.
- Support for the initiative comes from the Northwoods Protection Fund, created by Mary Griggs Burke after TPL helped conserve her family's property.
- In 2008, TPL conserves Long Island near writer Sigurd Olson's cabin at Burntside Lake, Minnesota.

SIDELIGHT
To prevent the probable development of a key access point to the Boundary Waters Canoe Area Wilderness, TPL purchases and razes a backwoods tavern known as the Chainsaw Sisters Saloon.

WHAT'S NEXT?
A future project will protect 9,000 acres in the home landscape of conservation legend Aldo Leopold.

Comprising parts of Minnesota, Wisconsin, and Michigan, the Midwest's Northwoods have been central to the region's economy, way of life, and imagination for generations. They have supported local economies and served as an outdoor playground for residents as well as visitors from across the nation. And we're just beginning to discover the woods' crucial role in addressing climate change—by removing carbon from the atmosphere and providing large intact landscapes for wildlife.

But with the timber industry on the wane and land values rising, the region's heritage is at risk, along with countless acres of wild landscape. Since the 1980s, The Trust for Public Land has been partnering with governments, civic leaders, businesses, and conservation groups to conserve highly developable inholdings within the region's national forests (especially lakefront land) and to prevent the breakup of private forests by protecting them with conservation easements that permit sustainable logging but pre-clude development. To date, TPL has protected more than 125,000 acres of the Northwoods.

This work intensified in 2000 with the inauguration of TPL's Northwoods Initiative, launched with the support of Mary Griggs Burke, a longtime Northwoods summer resident. TPL had helped Burke donate her 870-acre Forest Lodge property on Wisconsin's Lake Namakagon for conservation by the U.S. Forest Service. The century-old family lodge would become a Forest Service meeting site. As part of the arrangement, Griggs created TPL's Northwoods Land Protection Fund to support the initiative and acquire properties for eventual public ownership.

Of the more than 20 properties conserved to date with the help of the Northwoods Land Protection Fund, the one that most evokes the region's spirit may be Long Island in Burntside Lake near Ely, Minnesota. The lake's largest island is due north and in full view of Listening Point, the preserved writing cabin of pioneering Northwoods conservationist Sigurd Olson—a prolific author, powerful voice for wilderness, and primary shaper of the nation's 1964 Wilderness Act. Until recently, the Rome family owned Long Island, but when the family had to sell, development seemed imminent. "We couldn't have that," Jeff Rome told *Land&People* in 2007. Instead, TPL bought the land with the Northwoods Land Protection Fund and held it until federal funds permitted its conveyance to the Superior National Forest.

A paddler enjoys Burntside Lake, Minnesota. To date, TPL has protected more than 125,000 acres across the Midwest's Northwoods. Darcy Kiefel.

THE GAVIOTA COAST

Enjoying the beach at Ellwood Mesa, conserved in 2005. Community conservationists had long sought a way to protect the land. Rich Reid Photography.com.

"When we see a stretch of undeveloped coast like this, we tend to assume that it must already be protected, that it will remain wild and beautiful forever. That's not necessarily so."

—Debra Geiler,
former Southern California
director of TPL

Residents work for decades to protect—piece by piece—a visually and biologically unique stretch of southern California coastline.

WHERE: Santa Barbara County, California

YEARS: 2001–2008

HIGHLIGHTS

- In 2002, The Trust for Public Land acquires 2,500-acre El Capitan Ranch for California's Department of Parks and Recreation.
- Locals and TPL raise $20.4 million to protect Ellwood Mesa, a recreational paradise and winter home to monarch butterflies.
- Gaviota Village property added to Gaviota State Park in 2008.

SIDELIGHT
Schoolchildren created and raffled off a butterfly-design quilt to raise money for the Ellwood Mesa campaign.

West of Santa Barbara, the California coast stretches almost miraculously intact for mile after mile. Above remote beaches rise tall bluffs where hawks catch updrafts. Shorebirds crowd the water's edge, dolphins arc out of the ocean, and whales can be spotted farther offshore. Hikers, birdwatchers, picnickers, and water sports enthusiasts fit themselves into this wild environment with maximum pleasure and minimal impact.

The 30-mile-long Gaviota Coast (*gaviota* means "seagull" in Spanish) is a quintessential piece of California seacoast, and a rare one—it encompasses 50 percent of the remaining rural coastline in the southern part of the state. Here, as around the country, coastlands are prime targets for development. By 1999, residents of Santa Barbara County knew they had to act fast if they wanted to retain the Gaviota's natural character, and they began to organize. When the early goal of creating a national seashore on the coast proved unfeasible, residents proceeded—with help from The Trust for Public Land—to protect it one property at a time.

The first big victory came in 2002 when TPL acquired the 2,500-acre El Capitan Ranch for California's Department of Parks and Recreation, creating a link from El Capitan State Beach to the Los Padres National Forest via 11 miles of public trails winding from the shore up into the Santa Ynez Mountains. That transaction set the tone for local commitment to coastal preservation: a lead challenge gift prompted nearly 300 residents to donate and close the funding gap. On the heels of that success, an exciting opportunity arose to protect 137-acre Ellwood Mesa, a jewel at the Santa Barbara end of the coast where vernal pools shelter rare plants and animals, and eucalyptus groves attract up to 40,000 migrating monarch butterflies each winter.

TPL structured a transaction with the would-be developer, then worked with the local Friends of the Ellwood Coast and the City of Goleta to raise $20.4 million in public and private funding in just over two years. By then the community was well seasoned in raising funds and recruiting support. Schoolkids in butterfly costumes helped launch the campaign with a raffle. An artists' group sold paintings of the Ellwood property, a local couple asked their wedding guests to donate, and celebrities like singer Jackson Browne and ocean spokesman Jean-Michel Cousteau

lent their voices. Local philanthropists gave generously; in all, individuals contributed $8 million toward the goal. In 2005, the land was transferred to the City of Goleta, ensuring its protection as the Sperling Preserve.

The most recent piece of Gaviota coastline to be protected is the 43-acre parcel known as Gaviota Village, which had already been zoned for commercial development. Besides breathtaking ocean views, the property offers grassland, chaparral, and coastal sage scrub habitats, and its protection is part of a larger effort to consolidate up to 10,000 contiguous acres of wildlands and open space. Thanks in part to the leadership of U.S. Senator Dianne Feinstein in securing federal funds, TPL was able to protect the land in 2009 as an addition to the now 2,043-acre Gaviota State Park, at the western end of the coast.

So the chain of protected properties grows, but much work remains. As another key supporter, Congresswoman Lois Capps, told TPL, "Preserving this parcel is just the beginning in preserving the entire western gateway to this spectacular stretch of coastline we call the Gaviota."

Above: Children dressed as monarch butterflies to call attention to the Ellwood Mesa campaign. Rich Reid Photography. com. *Left: As many as 40,000 butterflies overwinter on the mesa each year.* Rich Reid Photography.com.

BONNEVILLE SHORELINE TRAIL

While Utah is blessed with a lot of wide open spaces, it is also the sixth most urbanized state in the nation—and most of its population lives in the Salt Lake Valley and along the Wasatch Front of the Rockies to the east. That's where The Trust for Public Land has been working to create the Bonneville Shoreline Trail, tracing the shoreline of prehistoric Lake Bonneville north to south through the Wasatch foothills. These lands had long been used by hikers, mountain bikers, equestrians, cross-country skiers, and families out for some fresh air, but booming development along the Wasatch Front led residents in the 1990s to envision a protected corridor that would keep them open for recreation. "It's now or never along the Wasatch Front," said then TPL project manager Margaret Eadington in a 1998 *Land&People* story. "Once these canyons are subdivided, public access to the mountains will be gone."

Working with local governments, conservation groups, the U.S. Forest Service, and Congress, TPL has been protecting properties for the trail since 1991. To date, more than 100 miles of trail have been protected in nearly 20 projects—most recently a 200-acre property in Weber County near North Ogden City, the first trail segment for that area. The ultimate goal is to complete a 280-mile trail that reaches from northern Utah into the heart of the state. The western writer/photographer Steve Trimble, whose family uses the trail nearly every day of the year (his son grew up mountain biking there) could be speaking for many when he writes, "In every season the Bonneville Shoreline Trail connects me with my home landscape and carries me into wildness."

Above: Since 1991, TPL has protected 100 miles along the trail, which serves the booming cities of the Salt Lake Valley. Stephen Trimble. *Right: The trail is a popular destination for snowshoeing and cross-country skiing.* Stephen Trimble.

"As growth continues, it is imperative that we continue to look for opportunities to secure access to the public lands along the Wasatch Front, so users can both access and enjoy their public lands."

—Brian Ferebee, former supervisor, Uinta-Wasatch-Cache National Forest

In a race with development, a magnificent recreation trail takes shape in the foothills along the fast-growing Wasatch Front.

WHERE: Northern Utah

YEARS: 1991–present

HIGHLIGHTS
- In 1991 the nonprofit Bonneville Shoreline Trail Committee is formed to promote the trail's construction.
- In 1997 the project receives its first federal funding: $500,000 from the Land and Water Conservation Fund.
- To date, The Trust for Public Land has helped protect more than 1,700 acres along the trail in more than 20 projects.
- The finished trail will traverse four counties and 40 communities along its projected 280-mile length.

SIDELIGHT
The prehistoric lake whose eastern boundary forms the trail was 1,000 feet deep and as large as Lake Michigan.

WHAT'S NEXT?
Additions to the trail totaling 1,850 acres are under option or in negotiation.

MOUNTAINS TO SOUND GREENWAY

The Trust for Public Land helps residents and local government plan and assemble a 100-mile ribbon of protected open space along heavily traveled I-90 southeast of Seattle.

WHERE: Western Washington State

YEARS: 1990–present

HIGHLIGHTS

• In 1990 the Issaquah Trail Club organizes an 85-mile march from Snoqualmie Pass to Puget Sound to promote a public greenway.

• With local groups and public agencies, TPL helps create the Mountains to Sound Greenway Trust and begins to option properties.

• To date, TPL has acquired 16,000 acres in 45-plus projects for the greenway.

SIDELIGHT

The Forest Legacy Program was created in the 1990 Farm Bill to help stem the loss of productive private forestland nationwide.

A family hikes at Snoqualmie Point along the Mountains to Sound Greenway, protected with TPL's help in 1995. Mountains to Sound Greenway Trust.

As Seattle and other Puget Sound communities began to boom in the 1980s, suburban sprawl spread southeast along the Interstate 90 corridor toward the Cascade Mountains. Trophy homes sprouted on bulldozed slopes where Douglas firs once grew; sleepy logging and mining towns gave way to office parks and shopping malls. Foreseeing that the region was at risk of losing its pristine wooded vistas and the easy access to nature and recreation that drew many transplants in the first place, conservationists began promoting the ambitious idea of a protected greenbelt from the Cascades to Seattle's waterfront—"mountains to sound."

In 1990, The Trust for Public Land teamed up with citizens' groups and public agencies to form the Mountains to Sound Greenway Trust, aiming to create a linked network of open space for 100 miles along I-90, preserving key natural and historic features within a framework of planned development and working forests. TPL started mapping and optioning key properties for protection, such as an 1,800-acre parcel owned by Weyerhaeuser Corporation at Rattlesnake Mountain, midway along the leafy corridor, and 260 acres at Snoqualmie Point that had already been subdivided for home sites. And the work has gone on ever since—with crucial support from the federal Forest Legacy Program and other public and private funds. Often the land is protected with easements that allow forestry to continue but prevent development. In all, TPL has helped protect nearly 16,000 acres along the Greenway in more than 30 projects, doing its part to ensure the long-term health of the region and to make one of the nation's busiest highways one of the most scenic as well.

MONTANA LEGACY

"The best legacies are the hardest to achieve. This project represents one of those rare chances to leave future generations one of the wildest places on Earth to use and enjoy for generations."

—Hansjörg Wyss, major donor to the Montana Legacy Project

Right: One goal of the project was to preserve forest-based jobs. Ted Wood. Below: Alex Love, son of TPL Northern Rockies director Deb Love, explores Holland Lake in Montana's Swan Valley. Deb Love.

In the largest transaction of its kind ever, The Trust for Public Land and The Nature Conservancy partner to forge a comprehensive conservation solution for Montana timberlands.

WHERE: Western Montana

YEARS: 1997–2010

HIGHLIGHTS

- Plum Creek Timber Company prepares to sell thousands of acres of forestlands, raising the prospect that development could threaten traditional uses and natural values.
- TPL and TNC partner with local communities and foundations to seek a large-scale solution.
- $100 million in private donations leverages $400 million in public funds to conserve 310,000 acres for wildlife, recreation, traditional uses, and working forests.

SIDELIGHT

The Swiss entrepreneur and donor who helped launch the project fell in love with the Rockies during a college summer job in 1958.

WHAT'S NEXT?

TPL is working to create a locally owned community forest for the Swan Valley community.

"Go big or go home." That, in essence, is the message delivered to conservationists and residents of Montana's Swan Valley by representatives of major foundations in 2006. Plum Creek Timber Company—the nation's largest private landowner and owner of forestlands across western Montana—had announced that 20,000 acres in the valley might be sold for development. But the potential funders believed that conservation groups needed to think beyond a single project to a comprehensive conservation solution for the valley and surrounding region—sometimes known as the Crown of the Continent ecosystem, the most intact biological ecosystem remaining in the contiguous United States. "Either protect the whole Swan Valley or we're not interested," Deb Love, The Trust for Public Land's Northern Rockies director, recalls them saying.

TPL had been protecting land in the valley of the Swan River since 1997, when it acquired 2,500 sensitive acres surrounding Lindbergh Lake from Plum Creek, eventually adding most of the lake's shorefront to the Flathead National Forest. It was part of a trend: private timberlands were being sold off piecemeal, raising the specter of development that would block wildlife corridors, disrupt habitat, and close lands to traditional local uses such as hunting, fishing, and recreation. Local officials and residents were growing deeply concerned about changes to their home landscapes. Over subsequent years, TPL worked with residents and local organizations to conserve other Plum Creek lands important to the community. But the pace was too slow, and even with another 20,000 acres protected, the region would be deeply at risk.

Because the foundations' challenge to think bigger was too much for any single conservation organization, TPL soon forged a partnership with The Nature Conservancy (TNC) to launch the largest project in TPL's history and the largest-ever U.S. conservation project of its type. The Montana Legacy Project, as it came to be known, would call on all the technical savvy and financial and political muscle the two groups could muster. Eventually, the deal grew to 310,000 acres—all the remaining Plum Creek acres in the Swan Valley and thousands more in other parts of western Montana, including many parcels identified by state and federal land managers as being critical for conservation. Most of the land would be protected in national and state forests. Some would remain working forests, contributing to local economies.

If the funders who had pledged to support the project were surprised by the size of the final package, they kept their word, with lead gifts totaling $40 million coming from the Wyss Foundation and the David and Lucile Packard Foundation. At the other end of the spectrum, an elementary school sent in honey-bear jars full of change (protecting grizzly bear habitat was one of the project's chief goals). Altogether, $100 million in private donations helped leverage $400 million in federal and state funding.

The Montana Legacy Project has been widely acclaimed as an example of community-based conservation done right, and a model for "large landscape conservation" nationwide. "At the end of the day," said The Nature Conservancy's Kat Imhoff in *Land&People*, "the only reason any of this is possible is that we all worked together."

A deer feeds on hay left out for horses in the Swan Valley. Montana Legacy was the largest conservation project of its kind in U.S. history. Ted Wood.

THE NORTHERN SIERRA NEVADA

"We have an opportunity here to make an incredible, lasting contribution to the ecological health and beauty of the Sierra—and beyond."

—David Sutton, director, TPL's Sierra Nevada program

"As the checkerboard project proceeds, I hope that we can consolidate large areas in public ownership so that management of those areas can be consistent, and that areas owned by private interests can continue to provide an economic engine for the Sierra in the form of sustainable logging."

—Jerry Tone, TPL national board member

Right: A hiker along the North Fork of the American River, a focus of TPL protection efforts. Phil Schermeister.

Over many years with many partners, The Trust for Public Land works to protect mountain lands vital for biodiversity, recreation, drinking water, and local economies.

WHERE: Northern Sierra Nevada, California

YEARS: 1975–present

HIGHLIGHTS
- From 1982 to1991, TPL helps protect 20,000-plus acres in scenic Hope Valley, south of Lake Tahoe.
- In 2003, TPL launches the Sierra Checkerboard Initiative, a five-year effort to consolidate landownership in the region.
- Through the Northern Sierra Partnership, born in 2007, TPL and other conservation groups leverage their resources to accomplish more in the Northern Sierra.

SIDELIGHT
A person hiking in the Sierra's checkerboard lands will pass from federally protected land to at-risk private land about every 1,800 steps.

Since the mid-1800s, Californians and visitors from around the globe have come to the lakes, meadows, conifer-draped slopes, and granite peaks of the Northern Sierra to play in the great outdoors, in all seasons, or just to enjoy the region's superlative scenery. Recreation aside, this mountain realm holds precious resources for people and other living things. The rivers that rise here provide drinking water for some 65 percent of Californians and for cities in Nevada. Half of the state's native plants are found in the Northern Sierra, as are 400 animal species, including an abundance and diversity of birds unsurpassed in the entire Sierra Nevada. The region's forests sequester large amounts of carbon to fight global warming, and its extensive, relatively intact habitat promises refuge for species as the climate changes.

As the San Francisco Bay Area's mountain playground, the Northern Sierra has long been a special focus of The Trust for Public Land. In the early 1980s, TPL learned that vacation-home development might soon come to Hope Valley, 15,000 acres of meadows and timbered uplands just east of Kit Carson Pass and south of Lake Tahoe. Since frontier days the valley had been lightly settled, much of it owned by Nevada ranchers who grazed their cattle there each summer. But as demand for recreation increased and the land's value for home sites grew, TPL began working with the

community, state and federal governments, and private donors to add valley lands to the surrounding national forest. Between 1982 and 1991, TPL helped protect more than 20,000 acres in and around Hope Valley, in 43 transactions.

In the years since, development pressure across the northern Sierra has only intensified, especially as some timberlands became more valuable for houses than for logging. The challenge of sustaining rural lifeways and protecting natural resources is complicated here by what's known as the "checkerboard" pattern of ownership—the legacy of a 19th-century federal policy that granted every other square-mile section of land to railroad companies. The checkerboard of alternating public and private lands hinders efforts to guide development, preserve land-based economies like forestry and recreation, conserve large contiguous tracts of wildlife habitat, fight wildfires, and protect watersheds.

In its 30-plus years of working in the Northern Sierra, TPL has conserved more land than any other conservation nonprofit—nearly 150,000 acres in more than 100 projects. Much of this work has focused on protecting lands in the checkerboard, along the Pacific Crest Trail, on the rivers that supply so much of the state's drinking water, and in valleys at high risk of inappropriate development. To advance its conservation goals, in 2007 TPL joined the

Northern Sierra Partnership (NSP), a consortium of conservation nonprofits, a business group, and two local land trusts that share strategies, leadership, donors, and funding in the interest of prioritizing and completing projects throughout the region.

Important recent projects include the conservation of 1,480-acre Waddle Ranch in the Martis Valley south of Truckee—the region's largest community—and the protection of almost 1,000 acres, including two high mountain lakes in the shadow of the iconic Sierra Buttes. And at the crest of the Northern Sierra—encompassing the high-elevation headwaters of the Middle Yuba, Little Truckee, and Feather Rivers—TPL recently protected more than 2,700 acres of checkerboard land through the first-ever conservation easement acquired from Sierra Pacific Industries, California's largest private landowner.

Recent projects at the Sierra Buttes, shown here reflected in Sardine Lake, brought land conserved by TPL in the Northern Sierra to nearly 150,000 acres. Rich Reid Photography.com.

LAND AND WATER

WATER IS ARGUABLY OUR MOST PRECIOUS natural resource. Clean water is critical to the health of America's communities and to the ecosystems that sustain both people and wildlife. And as anyone who has ever cast a line, launched a skiff, or taken a watery dip knows, our lakes, rivers, streams, and coastal waters are some of the nation's most beloved recreational sites. From coast to coast (and island to island), The Trust for Public Land works to safeguard vulnerable shorelines, wetlands, waterways, and watershed lands—and has been a leader among conservation groups in making the case for land conservation as a water protection strategy. Whether improving the water quality of a New Jersey bay, preserving an urban swimming hole in Texas, or adding a much-loved tropical beach to a Virgin Islands national park, The Trust for Public Land protects our life-giving waters for all to use and enjoy.

Kayaking near Pleasure House Point, Virginia, where the Lynnhaven River joins Chesapeake Bay. A current TPL project will protect the point, formerly slated for development. John Henley.

CARIBBEAN ISLANDS

"Development pressure on these islands makes it imperative to move as quickly as we can to protect their unique ecological, historic, cultural, and recreational resources."

—Greg Chelius, director, TPL's Florida and Caribbean office

Right: A fisherman mends his nets at San Miguel Natural Reserve, Puerto Rico. Angelo Cordero and Francis Davis. Below: TPL senior project manager Mildred Majoros at the reserve with a baby leatherback turtle. Pete Fodor.

On tropical islands that are both a vacation paradise and home to millions, The Trust for Public Land works to conserve special, often fragile, places for people and wildlife.

WHERE: U.S. Virgin Islands and Puerto Rico

YEARS: 1999–present

HIGHLIGHTS
- TPL tracks down far-flung heirs to add Big Maho Beach and surrounding lands to Virgin Islands National Park.
- Two important historic and natural sites on St. Croix are being protected with TPL's help.
- TPL helps create Puerto Rico's San Miguel Natural Reserve to protect the island's environment and create public access for its booming population.

SIDELIGHT
A private investigator hired by TPL finds the missing heir to Maho Bay Estate living in a California group home for Vietnam vets.

When does a conservation group need to hire a private detective? When the fate of a piece of paradise depends on tracking down a long-lost heir to that property. For nearly a decade, The Trust for Public Land had been negotiating with the 11 heirs of landowner Harvey Monroe Marsh to acquire Estate Maho Bay for the Virgin Islands National Park, on St. John. At 420 acres, the estate was the park's largest private inholding, its forested slopes a treasure trove of plant and animal diversity, including countless migratory birds and large nesting colonies of pelicans. Also on the property: the much-loved Big Maho Beach, one of the best in the Caribbean by some accounts, and by tradition open to island residents and visitors.

Time was running short to protect the estate and beach from private development, and acquiring them was complicated because all the heirs held the land jointly. TPL hoped to purchase all the owners' shares so it could transfer the land to the park. The key, it turned out, was finding one heir who lived in California and didn't even know about his legacy. With that share in hand and the help of a generous anonymous donor, TPL was able to acquire all the available shares of Estate Maho Bay and begin folding the land into the park as federal funds have become available. So now visitors to Big Maho Beach can continue to swim, snorkel, picnic, and watch sunsets as if they owned the place. Which they do.

Adding Estate Maho Bay to Virgin Islands National Park is one effort in TPL's vigorous program to conserve land for people in the Caribbean. On St. Croix, U.S. Virgin Islands, TPL is working to create a new national park at 1,400-acre Castle Nugent Farms.

This former cattle ranch hosts large populations of tropical birds and nesting grounds for sea turtles; just offshore is one of the nation's longest reef systems.

Just west of the Virgin Islands lies densely populated Puerto Rico, where TPL has partnered since 1999 with island families, public agencies, and local nonprofits to protect and create public access to forests, beaches, and watersheds. One important focus has been on conserving the lush tropical habitat of the island's Northeast Ecological Corridor—3,200 acres of sugar-sand beaches, coral reefs, mangrove wetlands, and forests that were growing when Columbus explored the island in 1493. The beaches here offer one of the most important nesting grounds in the United States for leatherback sea turtles. Since 2007, TPL has helped protect more than 540 acres there to create the San Miguel Natural Reserve. Project manager Mildred Majoros, who spent childhood summers on this coast, relishes the opportunity to protect her homeland. "What's special about working in Puerto Rico," she says, "is the sense of connection to the land."

Despite being privately owned, Big Maho Beach long has been popular with visitors to Virgin Islands National Park. TPL recently added the beach and hundreds of surrounding acres to the park.
Steve Simonsen.

BARTON SPRINGS POOL

The Barton Creek greenbelt winds deep into the heart of Austin, Texas, ending at Barton Springs Pool—a three-acre,1,000-foot-long swimming hole that draws more than a quarter-million visitors each year, to swim on hot days or laze on its grassy banks. Only three miles from the state capitol, Barton Springs Pool is to many Austin residents the soul of the city.

But as Austin boomed in the 1980s and '90s, concern grew that development upstream might be contributing to pollution of the underlying Edwards Aquifer, which feeds the spring and the pool. Concerned citizens had long urged more land protection, and that effort intensified after a spate of pool closings due to unsafe levels of bacteria. Austinites overwhelmingly approved a Save Our Springs (SOS) ordinance that set strict rules for new development, and The Trust for Public Land began partnering with the city to help conserve land upstream of the pool. Between 1993 and 1996, over four separate acquisitions, TPL assembled almost 1,000 acres of the most vulnerable land to help create the Barton Creek Wilderness Park. Easily reached from downtown, this major urban wildland conserves habitat for endangered species, preserves the area's dramatic views, and expands hiking trails and picnic areas.

Above: Mountain bikers take a break in Austin's Barton Creek Wilderness Park, created with TPL's help in the 1990s. Darcy Kiefel. Right: TPL archives.

"It's a great window for environmental education. Schoolkids can learn about the aquifer by seeing the recharge features, or the history of Austin from the old wagon-wheel tracks."

—Butch Smith, senior planner, Austin Parks and Recreation

Responding to concern that Austin might lose its spring-fed swimming hole, The Trust for Public Land helps create an urban wilderness park to protect it.

WHERE: Austin, Texas

YEARS: 1993–1996

HIGHLIGHTS
* In the late 1980s, high levels of bacteria force the repeated closing of Barton Springs Pool.
* Austin voters approve a Save Our Springs ordinance in 1990 and a $20 million bond to purchase land for the wilderness park in 1992.
* From 1993 to 1996, TPL acquires nearly 1,000 acres for the park.
* In several key projects, TPL protects other lands overlying the Edwards Aquifer.

SIDELIGHT
Native Americans, whose ancestors inhabited the area 11,000 years ago, call springs like Barton Springs the "eyes of the earth."

The Barton Creek projects are among several dozen TPL has completed with the City of Austin and Travis County to help create parks and greenways in the rapidly developing region. And in 2006, TPL's Conservation Vision team completed a comprehensive greenprint for Travis County. Other TPL projects to protect the sensitive Edwards Aquifer—which directly serves about two million people—include efforts that have helped create the Balcones Canyonlands Preserve near Austin and the Government Canyon State Natural Area near San Antonio.

Declining water quality in the Barton Springs Pool highlighted the need to protect land from development along Barton Creek. Eric Swanson.

EBEY'S LANDING NATIONAL HISTORICAL RESERVE

Built with TPL's help, Ebey's Landing National Historical Reserve preserves the natural beauty and agricultural heritage of Whidbey Island, Washington. Steph Taylor.

"The work of TPL and NPS to protect the Engle Farm is vitally important to our heritage, our economy, and the legacy we leave."

—Nancy Conard, former mayor of Coupeville

The Trust for Public Land helps farmers, local residents, and the National Park Service create a unique natural and agricultural reserve on a Puget Sound island.

WHERE: Whidbey Island, Washington

YEARS: 1984–2001

HIGHLIGHTS

- Whidbey Island residents petition Congress to protect their agricultural heritage in the Ebey's Landing National Historical Reserve, created in 1978.
- In 1984, TPL helps residents create the Whidbey-Camano Land Trust to protect land inside and outside the reserve, then helps it conserve land along the reserve's coastal trail.
- TPL in the 1990s acquires a historic farm, adding more than 300 acres of prairie to the reserve.

SIDELIGHT
The rich farm fields of Ebey's Prairie once held the world record for bushels of wheat raised on nonirrigated land.

An angular, 35-mile-long fishhook at the mouth of Puget Sound, Whidbey Island is barely an hour from Seattle but a world away in feeling—especially in its rural midsection, where a vast sweep of prairie, the remains of a prehistoric lakebed, rolls up to the edge of the sea at Ebey's Landing. This rich farmland has been worked for centuries, a unique agricultural heritage that is now part of 17,000-acre Ebey's Landing National Historical Reserve. Established by Congress in 1978, the reserve encompasses the historic town of Coupeville, two state parks, and more than 5,000 acres of natural prairie.

But protecting land within the reserve depends in part on local action, and in 1983 residents asked The Trust for Public Land for information about how to set up a local land trust. TPL land trust experts Jennie Gerard and Craig Lee presented to the group, which soon formed the Whidbey Camano Land Trust to conserve farms and natural land both inside and beyond the reserve boundary. That same year, TPL and the local land trust collaborated on its first project, protecting 60 acres bordering the National Park Service coastal trail through the reserve.

In the late 1990s, TPL answered the call to help protect one of the oldest farms on the Whidbey Island prairie. Boasting spectacular views of Puget Sound, Mt. Rainier, and the Olympic Mountains, the 415-acre Engle Farm had been farmed for 150 years, and the owners had no wish to stop. But they were facing bankruptcy, caught in a squeeze between rising land values driven by development and weak prices for farm products. "The land stood to be subdivided and sold," said Stephanie Taylor, who then headed TPL's work on Whidbey Island.

Working over six years with the Engles, local conservationists, national nonprofits, and state and federal officials, TPL successfully transferred much of the land to the National Park Service. The Engles were able to continue farming 111 acres, protected from development with a conservation easement. "We've never made a lot of money ansd probably never will," said Bob Engle in a 2002 *Land & People* story, "but ... we've got a connection to this earth."

THE CONNECTICUT RIVER WATERSHED

The Trust for Public Land partners with government, other conservationists, and community groups to conserve a watershed at the heart of New England.

WHERE: New Hampshire, Vermont, Massachusetts, and Connecticut

YEARS: 2004–present

HIGHLIGHTS
* In 2003, TPL helps conserve 126,000 acres around the river's headwater lakes, protecting water quality and the local economy.
* Launched in 2004, TPL's Connecticut River Program works to protect the river and its surrounding landscapes.
* To date, TPL has conserved more than 170,000 acres in the watershed, including land for the Silvio O. Conte National Fish and Wildlife Refuge.

SIDELIGHT
The river's name comes from the Algonquin *quinnetukut*, meaning "long tidal river," reflecting the ocean's influence on water levels far upstream.

The Connecticut is New England's great river, its 410 miles draining a 7.2-million-acre watershed that runs from headwaters at the Canadian border to Long Island Sound, through nearly every variant of the New England landscape. The river supports wildlife, farming, forests, fresh water, and recreation in New Hampshire, Vermont, Massachusetts, and Connecticut—and shapes the distinctive character of the communities it traverses.

In 2004, The Trust for Public Land established its Connecticut River Program to conserve land along the river and its tributaries. Goals of the program include preserving prime farmland for New England's food system, setting aside community forests and recreation areas, and protecting water resources that are important for recreation, native trout, and ultimately, the water quality of Long Island Sound. To further this mission, in 2007 TPL published *Conserving the Heart of New England: The Connecticut River Watershed*, a comprehensive report that highlights the watershed's resources and opportunities for conservation.

The program's launch was inspired in part by a long track record of success in the watershed and, in particular, by the successful completion of the Connecticut Lakes Headwaters project in

far northern New Hampshire in 2001. Here, International Paper had announced plans to dispose of 171,000 heavily forested acres, 126,000 acres of which drain to a series of headwater lakes and then to the Connecticut River itself. With potential development threatening this pristine water source, TPL gathered key partners, purchased the huge property—approximately 3 percent of the state—and held it until a conservation solution could be crafted and federal, state, and private funding secured. Most of the land was protected under a sustainable forestry easement and remains open for recreation, generating economic support for its communities.

Downstream, TPL has completed projects in every state along the river, protecting more than 170,000 acres in the watershed, from remote forests to urban farms. One important focus has been working with other conservation groups, Congress, and the U.S. Fish and Wildlife Service to assemble the Silvio O. Conte National Fish and Wildlife Refuge, which safeguards wildlife habitat along the river and its tributaries. In 2012, U.S. Secretary of the Interior Ken Salazar cited cooperative conservation along the river—in particular the work to build the Conte refuge—as an important reason for designating the Connecticut River watershed the nation's first National Blueway.

> "The Connecticut River Watershed is a model for how communities can integrate their land and water stewardship efforts with an emphasis on 'source-to-sea' watershed conservation."
>
> —Ken Salazar,
> U.S. secretary of the interior

The Connecticut River at South Newbury, Vermont. TPL focuses on protecting farmland, water resources, and community open space in the watershed—more than 170,000 acres so far. Jerry and Marcy Monkman/EcoPhotography.

CHATTAHOOCHEE RIVER CONSERVATION PROGRAM

Above: The Chattahoochee River is both a recreation destination and a source of drinking water for millions of Georgians. Darcy Kiefel. *Right: Children enjoy the river at Valley, Alabama.* Darcy Kiefel.

"It's kind of an amazing thing to me to think that we're just average citizens—and we can really save a piece of Georgia."

—Tuck Tucker, founder of a citizens' group to protect land on the Chattahoochee near Roswell

A river runs through fast-growing Georgia, its natural and recreational values the focus of a long-term protection campaign by The Trust for Public Land.

WHERE: Metro Atlanta and northern Georgia

YEARS: 1998–present

HIGHLIGHTS
* In 1998, TPL launches an ambitious initiative to protect drinking water, scenic and historic sites, and recreation access on the Chattahoochee River.
* TPL partners on the long-term effort with the National Park Service, conservation groups, the state, major foundations, and local businesses and individuals.
* More than $143 million in funding is raised, and more than 16,000 acres are conserved, including 76 miles of river frontage.

SIDELIGHT
TPL arranges for the heirs of a former Georgia governor to donate his 170-acre mountain farm—including an Indian mound, a Victorian mansion, and a mile of riverfront—to the state.

For metro Atlanta, and much of north central Georgia, the Chattahoochee River is the premier close-to-home natural resource—as the Columbia Gorge is to Portland or the Cuyahoga River to the Cleveland area. The river affectionately known as the 'Hooch rises in the southern Appalachians and flows southwest for 400 miles, through Atlanta's teeming suburbs to Alabama (where it forms most of the border between the two states), before entering the Florida panhandle and finally emptying into the Gulf of Mexico. Along the way, it supplies drinking water to half of Georgia residents—including 70 percent of metro Atlanta—as well as water for irrigation and industry. Not to mention recreation: the river's headwaters, from Helen to Lake Lanier, are popular for trout fishing and whitewater canoeing, kayaking, and other paddle sports. Each year more than three million visitors "hit the 'Hooch" for fishing, tubing, float trips, picnicking, hiking, visiting historic sites, or just to sit and watch the river flow by.

These have been troubled waters, though, as metro Atlanta's sprawl has devoured untold acres of rolling green countryside, bringing with it the whole complex of pollution problems related to development. The Chattahoochee has been regularly named one of the nation's ten most endangered rivers by the group American Rivers. In the 1990s, people living along the river began to organize on behalf of improving water quality, or saving beloved pieces of riverside land. Scattered parts of the river were already federally protected in the Chattahoochee River National Recreation Area (CRNRA), but much of the 6,500 acres authorized by Congress in 1978 had yet to be acquired.

A big vision for the Chattahoochee was needed, and it came from The Trust for Public Land, which in 1998 launched the Chattahoochee River Land Protection Campaign: a long-term effort to build a greenway along the river, from the headwaters downstream through Atlanta to Columbus in central Georgia. Partners in the effort included the National Park Service, Georgia's Department of Natural Resources, The Nature Conservancy, and The Woodruff Foundation; also critical was the work of TPL's staff in recruiting support and funding from Atlanta's civic and business leaders. They had to move fast in Atlanta's hot real-estate market. "We were competing with developers who wanted to build a luxury subdivision," says Rand Wentworth, then head of TPL's Atlanta office, about one key acquisition. Later, TPL helped communities on tributaries of the 'Hooch create greenprint plans to identify and acquire important lands.

So far, TPL's 15 years of conserving land along the Chatta-hoochee—including land for the CRNRA—have paid off in a big way. More than $140 million in private and public funding has been raised, and with support from generous donors and public partners, TPL and its partners have protected more than 16,000 acres along the river, including 76 miles of river frontage. The projects have been many and varied. Suburban residents of Roswell, just north of Atlanta, enlisted TPL's help to save a treasured riverfront tract from development for townhomes. A longtime river outfitter in the headwaters sold two properties to TPL; they were conveyed to the state to ensure perpetual public access for paddlers. In all, nearly eight contiguous miles of riverfront have been protected below Lake Lanier, in the most pristine section of the national recreation area.

Georgia and Atlanta continue to grow, as does people's appreciation of the gifts of the Chattahoochee. So the campaign goes on: to ensure safe and clean drinking water; provide places for people to hike, bike, fish, and jog; protect natural habitat; and, as Rand Wentworth says, "to enhance the quality of life up and down the river."

A father teaches his son to fish at Hardley Creek Recreation Area southwest of Atlanta. TPL has helped conserve 16,000 acres and 76 miles of frontage on the Chattahoochee River. Darcy Kiefel.

BARNEGAT BAY

"Preserving open space is of the utmost importance to Ocean County. Conservation is further advanced when we work in partnership with such organizations as TPL."

—John C. Bartlett Jr.,
Ocean County board of freeholders

Right: TPL New Jersey advisory council members Lynn and Harry O'Mealia walk a beach at Barnegat Bay. Jim David. Below: Preparing for a sailboat race on the bay. George M. Aronson.

The Trust for Public Land works for nearly two decades to safeguard a fragile watershed for people, wildlife, and water quality.

WHERE: Barnegat Bay, New Jersey

YEARS: 1993–present

HIGHLIGHTS

- TPL's efforts in Barnegat Bay begin with protecting 429 acres for the Edwin B. Forsythe National Wildlife Refuge in 1993.
- In 1995, TPL publishes *The Century Plan*, detailing 100 high-priority sites around the bay for protection; by 2008 nearly one-third of the targeted acres are conserved.
- With GIS mapping and a greenprint developed in 2008, TPL and its partners reinvigorate their efforts.
- In all, TPL protects nearly 12,000 acres in 64 projects around the bay.

SIDELIGHT

After optioning the 120-acres Meadows property at Reedy Point, TPL helps neighbors clear trash from the site, so it could be added to the Forsythe Refuge rather than developed.

WHAT'S NEXT?

A planned acquisition of almost 300 acres in the headwaters of the Toms River will prevent the probable construction of 373 housing units there.

Less than an hour and a half's drive from Manhattan and just over the horizon from Atlantic City lies Barnegat Bay, a precious slice of saltwater on the New Jersey coast. Ribbons of sandy barrier island shield its 40-mile length from the Atlantic, and the watershed that feeds it stretches inland to the Jersey pinelands. The bay's waters are irreplaceable habitat for coastal species and a treasured playground for generations of human residents and visitors—but they and the quality of life they support have been imperiled by development. Especially at risk is the aquifer that feeds the shallow bay and supplies most of the region's drinking water.

For two decades now, The Trust for Public Land has led the charge to conserve vulnerable lands within the 425,000-acre Barnegat Bay watershed. This effort has spanned much of what TPL does: real estate transactions, community organizing, finding and raising funds for conservation, research and publishing, and more lately computer-assisted mapping and planning. In 1995, TPL published *The Century Plan*, which identified 100 high-priority sites around the bay for protection; since then, 24,000 of the acres highlighted in the report have been conserved (11,000 of them with TPL's help). Much of this land was added to the Edward B. Forsythe National Wildlife Refuge, which manages more than 43,000 acres in the sensitive watershed for migratory birds and other wildlife. Other parcels have been conserved by Ocean County with funding from its Natural Lands Trust Program, which raises an average of $10 million each year for land acquisitions.

In 2007, TPL turned to one of its newest tools: state-of-the-art GIS technology that is giving stakeholders a comprehensive view of the urgent challenges still facing the region. "Watershed protection has been a part of TPL's work for decades," says Breece Robertson, who directs the GIS program. "But the new GIS tools make it possible for us to translate the conservation desires of those who live in the watershed into dynamic maps." In a series of meetings in 2007 and 2008 with a steering committee representing government and private sectors, TPL staff captured key criteria for rating lands in the watershed, identified more than 25,000 priority acres for protection, and created a greenprint to guide future conservation work.

A new publication emerged from the greenprinting effort: *Barnegat Bay 2020: A Vision for the Future of Conservation.* With computerized information about conservation needs and goals that vastly exceeds what was available in 1995, it is a bible for the many individuals and groups working in water quality, park and recreation planning, land conservation, and smart growth. A key priority these days, as New Jersey Advisory Council member Lynn O'Mealia told *Land&People* in 2008, is "trying to educate people that what happens around the headwaters of the watershed also has an important impact on the bay."

To date, The Trust for Public Land has protected nearly 12,000 acres in 64 projects in the Barnegat Bay watershed. Project manger Kathy Haake, who has worked there for more than a decade, understands that it remains deeply threatened but believes in the power of TPL's partnership with the community to craft future conservation successes. "We know based on twenty-five years of experience that there is tremendous support for conservation here. People know that ... if they help protect land, they will be able to come back to it in ten, twenty, or fifty years and say to their kids or grandkids, 'We did that.'"

Top: Development encroaches on Good Luck Point in 1993. Over ensuing years, TPL helped conserve more than 780 acres on the point. Dwight Hiscano. Above: TPL's 1995 Century Plan detailed conservation opportunities in the Barnegat Bay Watershed.

HERITAGE LANDS

MUSEUMS AREN'T THE ONLY PLACES where you can come face to face with historic and cultural treasures. In every corner of the nation are buildings and landscapes of cultural importance—touchstones with the past that remind us of who we are as a people. These places contribute to regional character while telling stories that help build our own character. Unless they are protected by concerned stewards, it is too easy for these places to be used up, torn down, paved over, or thrown out, and once they are gone, the lessons they may hold for us are gone too. Whether it's helping Native Americans recover a lost homeland, securing the historic habitat of world-famous writer, or safeguarding the boyhood home of a martyred civil rights leader, The Trust for Public Land works with government, donors, preservation groups, and concerned citizens to preserve the places that link us to the past and prepare us for the future.

Chief Johnny Jackson fishes for salmon on the Columbia River at Lyle Point, Washington. In 2007, TPL completed a 15-year-long protection effort by transferring the traditional fishing spot to the Yakama Nation. Phil Schermeister.

MARTIN LUTHER KING, JR. NATIONAL HISTORIC SITE

"This neighborhood is not something we had pride in. We had pride in what it had been and what it could be."

—Mtamanika Youngblood, former president, Historic District Development Corporation

Above: TPL president Will Rogers, left, joins Rev. Martin Luther King's sister, Christine King Farris, and other dignitaries in celebrating the 2008 protection of the last home on the King birthplace block for the national historic site. Kim Link Photography. Right: Karen Clarke.

By buying a handful of homes in the district where Martin Luther King, Jr. grew up, The Trust for Public Land helps revive the neighborhood and create a national park in his honor.

WHERE: Atlanta, Georgia

YEARS: 1982–2009

HIGHLIGHTS

- To advance the prospects for a national historic site honoring Dr. King, The Trust for Public Land acquires five homes in the Sweet Auburn neighborhood.
- The homes become the heart of the Martin Luther King, Jr. National Historic Site, created in 1980.
- TPL acquires more than a dozen properties for the historic site, including, in 2008, the last remaining home on the block of Dr. King's birthplace.

SIDELIGHT

In 1995, TPL acquires and demolishes a former pen factory to provide land for a much-needed visitor center and parking lot for the historic site.

In October 2009, The Trust for Public Land and the National Park Service threw a block party to celebrate TPL's latest acquisition for the Martin Luther King, Jr. National Historic Site. The house at 523 Auburn Avenue was the last property needed to complete protection of the block that holds the birth home of the civil rights leader. During the celebration, students played double-dutch jump rope on the sidewalk, and longtime residents of the Sweet Auburn neighborhood—the thriving center of Atlanta's middle-class black community when King was growing up there in the 1930s—gathered to share memories of him and the past. Christine King Farris, King's sister, spoke at the event, noting, "This is living history. I saw some children, even some grandchildren of original residents here today."

The fact that Sweet Auburn is again beginning to thrive has more than a little to do with TPL's work there over the past 30-plus years. In the late 1970s, influential members of Congress supported the idea of a national park to honor Martin Luther King, Jr. in his home city of Atlanta. While the concept was authorized, the obstacles were many—chief among them that the area around his birthplace was in steep decline with key properties about to go under the wrecking ball. TPL quietly sent two employees from its New York office to negotiate the purchase of five well-worn, single-family homes along Auburn Avenue, on the same block as King's birthplace and boyhood home. Says Marty Rosen, who presided over the transaction as then president of TPL, "We stopped the demolition permits that had been issued to literally level some of those historic houses. The vision was to make this a historic district, to display the best of Reverend King's neighborhood when it was alive and vibrant."

In 1982, TPL donated those houses to the National Park Service. One would serve as the park headquarters and the others were renovated for affordable housing, their facades restored to the way they looked in King's youth. The restoration was a turning point for the neighborhood. Today more than a million visitors a year tour the historic site, making it both an economic boon and a source of enormous pride for Sweet Auburn and Atlanta. The historic site and a surrounding preservation district contain 67 historic buildings, most built between 1890 and 1910, including

Dr. King's birthplace, gravesite, and the Ebenezer Baptist Church, where he preached from 1960 until his death.

Over the next two decades, TPL helped purchase more than a dozen properties for the park, including land for a pedestrian greenway linking the King district to the nearby Jimmy Carter Presidential Center. The 2008 addition of 523 Auburn Avenue to the NHS was an important final step in preserving the neighborhood as Dr. King would have remembered it.

Schoolchildren tour historic homes in 1991. TPL's donation of five homes in 1982 kicked off two decades of work during which it purchased more than a dozen properties for the historic site. Peter Beney.

CHIEF JOSEPH RANCH

Nez Perce men survey their ancestral homelands in eastern Oregon, returned to tribal ownership in 1997. Phil Schermeister.

"You feel that gust of wind? That's the old people greeting us. That's the old people saying, 'Oh, we are glad you are here.'"

—Horace Axtell, Nez Perce,
at the dedication of
Hetes'wits Wetes

The Trust for Public Land helps restore to the Nez Perce Tribe its ancestral homeland after 120 years of exile.

WHERE: Wallowa County, Oregon

YEARS: 1992–1997

HIGHLIGHTS
- Over several years TPL forges consensus among federal agencies, local interests, and the tribe.
- TPL acquires a 10,300-acre ranch for the Nez Perce, who rename it *Hetes'wits Wetes*, "precious lands."
- The Bonneville Power Administration provides funding to protect wildlife habitat on the land.
- The project leads to the founding of TPL's Tribal & Native Lands Program.

SIDELIGHT
Chief Joseph's birthplace is said to be on or near the ranch property, and his father is buried south of the ranch.

On a wet, chilly morning in June 1997, 31 riders guided their Appaloosa horses through a hillside meadow in the Wallowa Mountains of northeast Oregon. It was exactly 120 years since their ancestors rode and walked into exile from these Nez Perce homelands during one of the nation's last Indian wars. On this day, the Nez Perce were celebrating their return—made possible when The Trust for Public Land acquired a 10,300-acre ranch in the Wallowas for ownership by the tribe. During an emotional dedication ceremony, Nez Perce elder Horace Axtell stood in a gentle rain overlooking Chief Joseph Canyon and named the newly acquired ranch *Hetes'wits Wetes*, or Precious Lands.

Chief Joseph and his band lived peacefully in these river valleys and mountains until 1877, when they were forced by the U.S. Army across the freezing Snake River, leaving behind the Oregon lands they and their forebears had inhabited for millennia. Then Joseph led a four-month, 1,200-mile fighting retreat through some of the West's roughest terrain before surrendering to save the starving remnant of his people. "I will fight no more forever," he famously said.

Conveying the former cattle ranch to the Nez Perce climaxed two years of complex negotiations with the landowner, Wallowa County, other local interests, and the federal Bonneville Power Administration (BPA). Because it was also precious homeland for bear, elk, bighorn sheep, salmon, and other wildlife, funds for the purchase came from the BPA—from a program to replace wildlife habitat lost to dams. The idea of restoring the land to the Nez Perce—its original inhabitants—made sense to everyone. "It was the perfect circle, the perfect endpoint for the ranch," said ranch owner Hans Magden in 1997. TPL later was able to add 6,000 acres to the protected homeland.

Since their repatriation, the Nez Perce have managed the land as a wildlife preserve. Yet beyond its lush meadows, sparkling creeks, and abundant wildlife, they perceive a spiritual dimension. The 300-plus people gathered for the dedication were seeking connections with their past and belief in their future. "The return of the Nez Perce to Hetes'wits Wetes for the first time in more than a century struck a deep chord in Americans ... and in people throughout the world," wrote former TPL vice president Bowen Blair, who led the conservation effort.

The project also led to the founding of The Trust for Public Land's Tribal & Native Lands program, which over the next decade protected more than 200,000 acres with and for Native people.

KEY WEST CUSTOM HOUSE

In the rapidly developing Florida Keys, The Trust for Public Land rescues a landmark public building that becomes a popular museum.

WHERE: Key West, Florida

YEAR: 1993

HIGHLIGHTS
- Built in 1891, the Key West Custom House witnessed the start of the Spanish-American war, the arrival of Cuban immigrants, and much more local history.
- When the historic red-brick structure was in danger of being torn down for development, TPL purchased it in 1993 and conveyed it to the State of Florida.
- The building is now home to the Key West Museum of Art & History at the Custom House.

SIDELIGHT
The Museum of Art & History houses memorabilia about Key West's most famous resident, Ernest Hemingway, including his bloodstained WWI uniform.

Left: A bronze statue of former Key West resident Ernest Hemingway outside the Custom House. Michael Wray. Below: Saved from destruction in 1993, the historic Key West Custom House today houses an art and history museum. Michael Wray.

The Trust for Public Land's work in the Florida Keys began in 1976, when it protected nearly 3,000 acres to help build the Great White Heron National Wildlife Refuge. To date, TPL has completed more than 30 conservation projects in this chain of islands off the southern tip of the Sunshine State—from precious lands added to the National Key Deer Refuge on Big Pine Key to properties on Middle Torch, Upper Sugarloaf, Knockemdown, Cudjoe, and No Name Keys.

But perhaps the most visible accomplishment came in the early 1990s, when the once-sleepy islands were imperiled by a rising tide of development. Not just natural lands but historic structures were at risk—including the beautiful red-brick Custom House in Key West. One of Florida's ten most architecturally significant buildings, the 1891 structure was the site of the inquiry into the sinking of the battleship *Maine*, the dramatic event that launched the Spanish-American War, and later served as a post office, a courthouse, and an immigration station for arrivals from Cuba. But before TPL came to its rescue, it was in decay, boarded up and abandoned, and slated to be torn down for a private yacht club.

Using funds from the Florida's Conservation and Recreation Lands (CARL) program, TPL purchased the Custom House and transferred it to the state. Today the fully restored building houses the Key West Museum of Art & History, one of the area's chief attractions, featuring exhibits about the town's well-known visual artists and its colorful history.

WAO KELE O PUNA

Above: Dancers celebrate the protection of Waimea Valley in 2006, one of TPL's 26 projects in Hawai'i. Suzanne Westerley. Right: Examining an 'ōhi'a lehua blossom at Wao Kele o Puna. Arna Photography.

"You cannot have Hawaiian culture without the interaction between the human native and the natives in nature. A forest like Wao Kele o Puna is one of our greatest shrines."

—Kekuhi Kanahele, a hula practitioner whose family has harvested plants from the forest for generations

After a long struggle, The Trust for Public Land helps restore a treasured rainforest to the native community that depends on it for physical and spiritual sustenance.

WHERE: Island of Hawai'i

YEARS: 2001–2006

HIGHLIGHTS
* In the 1980s, owners plan to lease land in the Wao Kele o Puna rainforest for geothermal drilling, sparking protests by Hawaiians and conservationists.
* At the Hawaiians' request, TPL negotiates to acquire the 28,000-acre property in 2006, with support from the state, private donors, and the federal Forest Legacy Program.
* TPL's Hawai'i Heritage Lands program protects sites important to Hawaiians' connection with their home landscapes.

SIDELIGHT
The 'ōhi'a lehua, central to Hawaiian folklore, is the only tree that can take root in fresh lava flows.

WHAT'S NEXT?
On O'ahu, TPL is helping a community nonprofit protect a five-acre property that includes petroglyphs and a heiau (place of worship) named after the first pahu (drum) brought from Tahiti to Hawai'i.

For more than 1,000 years, Native Hawaiians have hunted, foraged, and gathered medicinal plants in a 25,800-acre rainforest called Wao Kele o Puna, south of Hilo on the archipelago's Big Island. More than 100 native plant species are found within the forest, including 800-year-old 'ōhi'a lehua trees. "People go in there, generation after generation," said Hawaiian activist Palikapu Dedman in a 2006 Land & People story. "They use it, and they protect it."

But Native people didn't own (in the Western sense) Wao Kele o Puna. Along with many ancestral lands, it ended up in private hands after the 1893 overthrow of the Hawaiian kingdom by U.S. business interests. In the 1980s, though, plans to exploit this treasured land for geothermal energy sparked impassioned protests. The forest drapes over the shoulder of the Kīlauea volcano, home of the fire goddess Pele. To Native Hawaiians, drilling into the mountain would be a desecration, and conservationists and Hawaiians both feared that the drilling would disrupt the ecosystem of the state's last pristine lowland rainforest.

The Pele Defense Fund, on behalf of the activists, filed more than a dozen lawsuits against the project, in vain. After two test wells were drilled, protests escalated, eventually turning public opinion against the drilling, and the plan was abandoned in 1994. In subsequent developments, a state court upheld the Hawaiians' right to enter and use the forest, and the landowner decided to sell. Sensing a path to permanent protection of the land, the Pele Defense Fund contacted The Trust for Public Land for help in 2001. TPL was able to secure an agreement with the landowner and, over the next several years, worked to win support and funding from state and federal sources.

In July 2006, TPL acquired Wao Kele o Puna and transferred the forest to the Office of Hawaiian Affairs (OHA)—which administers lands held in trust for Native Hawaiians. It was the first major parcel of ceded land lost at the time of the kingdom's overthrow to be returned to Native Hawaiian control. Today the forest is managed by OHA and representatives from community associations in the rural subdivisions that surround it. As one community member said, at a celebratory meeting soon after the agreement to protect the land was announced: "It took everybody to save it, and it'll take everybody to manage it."

This landmark effort helped give rise to TPL's Hawai'i Heritage Lands program, which works to preserve and promote the islands' unique land-based culture and bring Hawaiians closer to the land.

Its projects are scattered around the islands. On Moloka'i, a partnership between TPL and the local Hālawa Valley Land Trust preserved a patchwork of *kalo* (taro) fields for traditional agriculture. On O'ahu, TPL helped OHA reacquire the 1,875-acre Waimea Valley, one of the last intact *ahupua'a* (a traditional mountain-to-sea land division) on the island and home to hundreds of Hawaiian cultural sites. TPL purchased 74 acres on the Hāna coast of Maui at Mū'olea Point, once the summer residence of Hawaiian king David Kalākaua. And back on the Big Island, TPL has protected land at several key historic and cultural sites, including Lapakahi State Historical Park and 238 acres of the Ki'ilae shoreline to expand the Pu'uhonua o Hōnaunau National Historical Park. In all, TPL has helped to protect more than 40,300 acres in 26 projects across the Hawaiian Islands.

Activists examine an abandoned geothermal wellhead at Wao Kele o Puna. Stopping geothermal development in the rainforest ultimately led to its protection by TPL and its ownership by the Office of Hawaiian Affairs. Phillip Rosenberg Photography.

EUCLID BEACH CAROUSEL

Above: The long-lost 1909 Euclid Beach Carousel, returned to Cleveland by TPL and due to reopen in 2013. TPL archives. Right: A carved horse and chariot, ready for the restoration. The Plain Dealer/Landov.

"The citizens who had worked so hard to try and save the carousel hugged each other in tears."

—From a report on the 1997 carousel purchase at auction in a TPL newsletter

F or nearly 60 years, a carousel built in 1909 was among the premier attractions at the private Euclid Beach Park on Lake Erie's shoreline near Cleveland. Until the park closed in 1969, going for a spin on the carousel—one of the oldest and finest ever made by the Philadelphia Toboggan Company, sporting 54 wooden horses and two elaborately carved chariots—was a beloved tradition for local families. Between 1981 and 1985, The Trust for Public Land worked with the city and state to acquire the former amusement park as a public beach, but by that time the fondly remembered carousel was well into its second life at an amusement park in Maine.

Then in 1997, the carousel again was put up for sale, and Cleveland preservationists asked TPL to try to buy it at auction and bring it home. (Not standard fare for a land conservation organization, perhaps, but clearly within TPL's transaction expertise.) Collectors journeyed to Maine from afar to vie for the antique carved horses. The collection could easily have been broken up and the horses sold separately, but in the second round of bidding former TPL vice president Kathy Blaha made the winning bid on the entire carousel. As reported in a TPL newsletter, "Even the collectors who had traveled thousands of miles to bid on individual horses cheered."

The early plan was to restore the carousel by the spring of 1999. That effort bogged down for lack of funding, and for years the horses and chariots have been stored at Cleveland's Western Reserve Historical Society. In 2010, that group, the Euclid Beach Carousel Society, and Euclid Beach Park Now—a nonprofit dedicated to preserving the park's history—launched a fundraising campaign to restore the horses and chariots and rebuild the carousel. In 2012 the historical society broke ground for a new glass pavilion to house the attraction in its history center at University Circle, and in 2013 the Euclid Beach Carousel is expected to reopen to a new generation of Cleveland families.

The Trust for Public Land buys a historic and much-loved carousel at auction so it can be restored to Cleveland's families.

WHERE: Cleveland, Ohio

YEAR: 1997

HIGHLIGHTS

- From 1909 to 1969, northern Ohio families come to ride on the beautifully carved carousel horses at Euclid Beach Park.
- In 1997, local preservationists ask TPL to buy the disassembled carousel at auction so it can be returned to Cleveland; TPL's winning bid is $715,000.
- A new partnership of the Western Reserve Historical Society and two nonprofits will restore and reopen the carousel by 2013.

SIDELIGHT

In the first round of bidding, one collector offered $42,500 for a single carved horse.

HYDE FARM

The Trust for Public Land's timely purchase of a historic riverside farm allows a farmer to stay on his land and preserves a reminder of metro Atlanta's rural roots.

WHERE: Cobb County, Georgia

YEARS: 1992–2010

HIGHLIGHTS
* For most of the 20th century, the Hyde family farms 120 acres in Marietta, north of Atlanta, on the Chattahoochee River.
* In 1992, TPL buys 40 acres of the farm for the Chattahoochee River National Recreation Area, averting the sale of the land to pay taxes.
* In 2010, TPL protects the final piece of Hyde Farm by conveying it to Cobb County and the National Park Service.

SIDELIGHT
For a time the Hydes supported themselves by keeping milk cows and growing sugarcane, which a neighbor boiled down into syrup.

J. C. Hyde was 11 in 1920, when his father bought a 120-acre farm on the Chattahoochee River near Marietta, Georgia. J. C., his brother, Buck, their parents, and four sisters moved into a cabin built in the 1840s. Today Marietta is an upscale suburb north of Atlanta, and the 19th-century farm is encompassed by subdivisions. How these acres continue to exist as farmland is a tale of faithfulness to family, the land, and the grail of maintaining open space around one of the nation's fastest-growing metro areas.

The father and two brothers, both bachelors, farmed the land all their lives, growing a wide array of livestock and crops including sweet potatoes, okra, corn, and tomatoes. They worked the heavy red-clay soil with mules because motorized equipment compacted it. Before Hyde Senior died, J. C. and Buck promised him they would never sell the farm. But in 1987, Buck died suddenly, and the government—appraising the riverfront land for development—presented J. C. with an inheritance tax bill of more than $500,000. It seemed to J. C. that he had no choice but to sell at least part of the farm to pay the taxes.

Until, in 1992, The Trust for Public Land offered him an alternative. TPL would buy 40 riverfront acres of the farm for addition to the Chattahoochee River National Recreation Area, which protects land along a 48-mile stretch of the river north of Atlanta. (See page 128.) The transaction enabled J. C. to pay his taxes and remain on the farm during his lifetime, and it gave TPL the right of first offer to purchase the balance of the land when he died. "Fortunately, J. C. loves his land and wanted to see it protected," said Rand Wentworth, then head of TPL's Atlanta office, in a 2000 *Land&People* story.

J. C. went back to farming with his mule, Nell, and lived on the farm he loved until near the time of his death in 2004. That year, TPL began working acquire the rest of the Hyde Farm, complete with its 19th-century cabin and outbuildings, as a historic site to be managed jointly by local Cobb County and the National Park Service. Under a recent arrangement with the nonprofit Cobb Landmarks and Historical Society, students from the University of Georgia have been studying Hyde Farm's past—including its farm terraces that remain intact from the early 1900s—to help determine how the park can best be used in the future. Part of the university's research is aimed at finding heirloom fruits and vegetables to grow there, which could include green beans, cabbages, apples, pears, and peaches, along with the currently farmed sweet potatoes. "If it's a viable farm, then it could be a source for farmers markets," said Cari Goetcheus, an associate professor at UGA's College of Environment and Design, in a 2012 article in the *Marietta Journal*.

"It's a very treasured and very special place."

—Cari Goetcheus, associate professor, University of Georgia College of Environment and Design

"I think it's the happiest life there is, on a farm."

—J. C. Hyde to a reporter for *Land&People* magazine

With TPL's help, Georgia farmer J. C. Hyde was able to keep his promise to his father and stay on his land. Nick Arroyo.

WALDEN WOODS

Above and right: Children peek into a replica of Henry David Thoreau's cabin at Walden Pond in Concord, Massachusetts. John Suiter. Opposite: Walden Pond in fall. Susan Lapides.

"A man is rich in proportion to the number of things he can afford to let alone."

—Henry David Thoreau

A landscape immortalized by Henry David Thoreau is preserved so that visitors can experience it as the writer did.

WHERE: Concord, Massachusetts

YEARS: 1990–1994

HIGHLIGHTS

- The Trust for Public Land acquires land near Walden Pond to prevent its imminent development.
- Rock musicians, prominent politicians, and foundations rally to raise funds for the Walden Woods Project.
- Acquisitions include a historic home as headquarters for the educational Thoreau Center.

SIDELIGHT

Because one of the planned developments would have included affordable housing, TPL and the Walden Woods Project purchased an alternative housing site and gave it to the town.

Some places are important to Americans because battles were fought there, great leaders were born there, or history was made there. Others are important because they stand for an idea that is central to how we see ourselves. Foremost among these are the woods and pond in Concord, Massachusetts, where Henry David Thoreau lived from 1845 to 1847, tramping the country and forming observations that would influence the world. His *Walden, or Life in the Woods* became the classic American statement on the powers of straight thinking, independence, and wild retreat.

Its proximity to Boston made Walden Pond a convenient pilgrimage site—especially after Thoreau was rediscovered as a back-to-nature icon in the 1960s. City-weary Bostonians and visitors from around the world came to swim in the pond, visit Thoreau's reconstructed cabin, or just soak up his spirit in the surrounding woods. But few visitors realized that, while the pond and a small rim of land around it belonged to a state reservation, most of the woods were in private hands. This led the National Trust for Historic Preservation to list Walden as one of the nation's 11 most endangered historic sites.

In the late 1980s the threat became tangible when authorities approved two development projects in the heart of Walden Woods: a 25-acre, 139-unit condominium cluster and a 400,000-square-foot office park. To many, the prospect seemed like sacrilege. As the novelist E. L. Doctorow wrote in an essay published in *Land&People,* "… these woods … stand transformed by Thoreau's attention into a kind of chapel in which this stubborn Yankee holy man came to his and, as it turns out, our redemptive vision. So there is a crucial connect of American clay and spirit here:

If we neglect or deface or degrade Walden, the place, we sever a connection to ourselves."

Fortunately Doctorow wasn't the only influential person to feel this way. A coalition of politicians, writers, and entertainers soon formed the Walden Woods Project to work for the land's protection. Rock musician Don Henley of the Eagles—a leader of the effort—staged benefit concerts featuring performers such as Bonnie Raitt, Jimmy Buffett, and Arlo Guthrie. Gifts, large and small, started to pour in from Thoreau admirers around the nation.

In 1990 Henley approached The Trust for Public Land. He wanted to know if TPL could negotiate with the developers and hold the land until enough money was in hand to protect it. Beginning in 1991, TPL protected 112 acres with the Walden Woods Project, including Bear Garden Hill, where Thoreau liked to take moonlight walks, and a parcel containing a historic home that has been transformed into a library and program site for the Thoreau Institute, which promotes the writer's work and legacy.

Some of the land was added to Walden Pond State Reservation, which today spans 462 acres. Pilgrims continue to flock to the site, and many of them bring their children, hoping to pass on Thoreau's legacy to the next generation. Of all the reasons why it was important to keep Walden as Thoreau knew it, this is a big one. As Doctorow wrote, "You have to be able to take the children there, and to say 'This is it, this is the wood Henry wrote about. You see?'"

"Walden is the material out of which Thoreau made his book— as surely as he made his house from the trees he cut there, he made his book from the life he lived there."

—E. L. Doctorow

AMERICAN BEACH

"A remarkable piece of American history and culture, American Beach is also a beautiful natural resource ... protected for generations to come."

—Susan Grandin, former director, TPL's Northeast Florida Office

Right: MaVynee Betsch worked for years to protect the historic African-American beach resort founded by her great-grandfather. Regis Lefebure. Below: American Beach in about 1950. Courtesy Amelia Island Museum of History.

A storied recreation spot for African-Americans on the northeast Florida coast becomes a historic park thanks to a colorful champion and The Trust for Public Land.

WHERE: American Beach, near Jacksonville, Florida

YEARS: 2004-2005

HIGHLIGHTS
- In the segregated 1930s, black entrepreneur A. L. Lewis buys 200 seaside acres north of Jacksonville to build a resort for his employees and other African-Americans.
- Lewis's great-granddaughter, MaVynee Betsch, recruits support to protect American Beach and its historic buildings.
- In 2004, TPL acquires two properties in a $2.275 million transaction with Nassau County, preserving 200 feet of prime beachfront property, a multifamily residence, and the legendary Evans Rendezvous nightclub.

SIDELIGHT
When fully restored, Evans Rendezvous will be the only oceanfront public building in northeast Florida.

In the Jim Crow South of the 1930s, most Florida beaches were closed to African-Americans. So the enterprising Abraham Lincoln Lewis, president of the Afro-American Insurance Company and Florida's first black millionaire, bought 200 acres of prime beachfront on Amelia Island, north of Jacksonville, and helped found the resort town of American Beach as a seaside getaway for his employees. Through the 1950s, American Beach was the place to be for fun and entertainment. Black families could own property there for full-time residence or weekend escapes, and the black cultural elite flocked to its hotels, restaurants, and nightclubs. One of the latter, Evans Rendezvous, was an important anchor of the community, welcoming such notables as Ray Charles, Cab Calloway, and Louis Armstrong.

When development began to encroach on the town, American Beach found its champion in Lewis's great-granddaughter, the flamboyant and determined MaVynee (pronounced "mah-VEEN") Betsch, aka the "Beach Lady." An artist, performer, and opera singer by training, she called on all her eloquence and theatrical style to protect her beloved beach, Evans Rendezvous, and nearby historic homes, marshaling supporters and partners and promoting her cause in newspapers and magazines nationwide.

Among those partners was The Trust for Public Land, which in 2004 purchased 200 feet of beachfront and Evans Rendezvous, then helped local Nassau County raise full funding from the Florida Communities Trust to acquire the property. The land is now the American Beach Historic Park. The historic nightclub is slated to become a cultural center, and Betsch, who died in 2005, will be remembered by a plaque in the building. She lived to see the last remaining large dune at American Beach, which she had named NaNa ("grandmother" in the West African Tiwi dialect), transferred to the National Park Services's nearby Timucuan Ecological and Historic Preserve.

BROWN V. BOARD OF EDUCATION NATIONAL HISTORIC SITE

The Trust for Public Land helps create a new historic site interpreting the impact of the landmark Supreme Court decision outlawing school segregation by race.

WHERE: Monroe School, Topeka, Kansas

YEAR: 1993

HIGHLIGHTS

- In 1950, 20 children in Topeka are refused admission to their closest neighborhood school; their parents join a lawsuit brought by the NAACP.
- In *Brown v. Board of Education,* the Supreme Court rules unanimously that segregated public education is unconstitutional, fueling the civil rights movement in all areas of society.
- In 1993, TPL purchases the Monroe School in Topeka, saving it from demolition, and conveys it to the National Park Service.
- The transformed school building opens as a national historic site in 2004.

SIDELIGHT

The *Brown v. Board of Education* U.S. Supreme Court case involved more than 150 plaintiffs from five states.

An anonymous two-story brick-and-stone schoolhouse in Topeka, Kansas, became an icon of the Civil Rights movement following the landmark 1954 Supreme Court decision that finally outlawed segregation in America's public schools. For decades African-American parents had been protesting the Kansas law that allowed large cities to operate separate schools for blacks and whites, and Monroe School was one of two segregated Topeka schools cited in their most recent lawsuit. Faced with five such suits from around the country, the Supreme Court consolidated them under one name, *Oliver Brown et al. v. the Board of Education of Topeka.* Brown, a minister, was one of the Topeka parents, and Monroe School, as it happened, was the school that his daughter attended.

So it seemed a logical place for the National Park Service to establish a historic site recognizing the groundbreaking nature of the *Brown v. Board* decision and explaining the history of the school segregation—not just in Topeka but nationwide. But by 1993, the deteriorating old school building was in danger of being torn down, despite having been declared a National Historic Landmark and the fervent efforts of residents—including Oliver Brown's

adult children—to save it for its historical value. So The Trust for Public Land stepped in and bought the building until the National Park Service could acquire it.

After several years of renovation and preparation, the historic site opened in 2004—the 50th anniversary of the court decision—with exhibits interpreting the case and its impact on the nation. It features an auditorium with continuous film screenings, an Education and Justice gallery (in the former kindergarten classroom), information kiosks, and music stations, as well as special exhibits. In 2012, the park launched Brown v. Board of Education Oral History Project to capture the stories of community members that relate to the historic Brown decision.

"The Brown v. Board of Education National Historic Site will forever symbolize both the harsh realities of segregation and the promise of equality embodied in the Fourteenth Amendment to the Constitution," wrote Brown family member Cheryl Brown Henderson in a 1994 *Land&People* article about the protection effort. "It demonstrates a commitment to a more representative National Park System in which Americans of all racial and ethnic backgrounds can take pride."

"We conclude that in the field of public education the doctrine of 'Separate but Equal' has no place. Separate educational facilities are inherently unequal."

—Chief Justice Earl Warren for a unanimous U.S. Supreme Court, May 17, 1954

Once at the center of an epic school desegregation decision, Monroe School is today a national historic site. Phil Schermeister.

WORKING LANDS

THE NATION'S FARMS, RANCHES, AND WOODLANDS yield food and timber, shelter wildlife, safeguard clean water, sustain local economies, and comprise some of our most beautiful landscapes. A working landscape may be a Western forest of tens of thousands of acres, an emerald mosaic of ranchland in the shadow of the Rocky Mountains, or the last farm in a New England town, supplying healthy food while linking the community to its rural past. Such lands are too important to be lost to poorly planned development. The Trust for Public Land works with landowners, agencies, and communities to keep working lands working while preserving their environmental benefits—often through the use of conservation easements that prevent development while permitting ranching, farming, and sustainable forestry to continue. The result: lands that continue to support our bodies, industries, spirits, and communities—along with rural ways of life that have endured for generations.

A cornfield in Pepperell, Massachusetts, protected as part of a 2008 TPL conservation project. Preserving farmland was one goal of the project, and an easement held by the town specifically allows agriculture to continue.
Jerry and Marcy Monkman/EcoPhotography.

MAʻO ORGANIC FARMS

Above: Interns at MAʻO Farms on Oʻahu learn all aspects of organic farming and receive a community college education. Arna Photography. Right: TPL staffers Laura Hokunani Edmunds Kaʻakua, left, and Lea Hong with MAʻO produce. Christina Aiu.

"I've heard about all that's going on here for years and years . . . so I jumped at the opportunity to come and not just see for myself but also to allow the world to see what you all are doing."

—Michelle Obama, during her visit to MAʻO Farms

An organic farm nurtures good food, Hawaiian youth, and *aloha ʻāina*—love of the land.

WHERE: Oʻahu, Hawaiʻi

YEARS: 2007–2010

HIGHLIGHTS
- In 2001 Hawaiian community activist Kukui Maunakea-Forth and her husband found a program for Oʻahu's youth combining farming with academics and leadership training.
- From 2007 to 2010, The Trust for Public Land helps expand MAʻO Farms from less than 4 acres to 23 acres by acquiring adjacent land.
- First Lady Michelle Obama visits MAʻO Farms in 2011 and speaks to the student farmers.

SIDELIGHT
MAʻO Farms' T-shirts and the boxes that hold its organic greens bear the motto: "No panic, Go organic."

Oʻahu's leeward coast is home to one of the largest Native Hawaiian populations in the islands—and some of the nation's highest rates of obesity and diabetes, partly due to the limited accessibility of fresh, nutritious food. But MAʻO Organic Farms, in the Lualualei Valley northwest of Honolulu, is working to change that. MAʻO is an acronym for the farm's full name, Māla ʻAi ʻŌpio—"youth food garden." Every year MAʻO enrolls motivated high school graduates—most from at-risk backgrounds—in a two-year Youth Leadership Training internship. Students work three days a week while attending community college, learning every stage of the organic farming industry: from planting and harvesting to packaging and sales. The produce they grow is sold at farmers' markets and featured at many of Honolulu's top restaurants, and the farm has a growing community-supported agriculture (CSA) program; income from these sales supports its educational endeavors.

For several years after MAʻO's founding in 2001, its reach was limited by its tiny size: less than four acres. So in 2007 and 2008, The Trust for Public Land helped MAʻO Farms acquire an 11-acre chicken farm next door, and helped the program add another 7.5 acres in 2010, making it the largest organic farm in the state. The added land enables MAʻO Farms to grow more food and serve more young people. In 2011, First Lady Michelle Obama toured the farm as part of her Let's Move! campaign, highlighting it as a model for increasing awareness of—and access to—healthy eating options.

One goal of MAʻO Organic Farms is to promote self-sufficiency and a closer relationship to the land, as expressed in the Hawaiian phrase *aloha ʻāina*—roughly translated as "love of the land." But its larger ambition is to raise a new generation of youth leaders for their community. Many interns are the first in their family to attend college, and several have graduated. "We are going back to our roots—literally," said intern Michelle Arasato in a 2012 *Land&People* story. "For the Hawaiians, everything was put into the *ʻāina*. You have to take care of it so that it will produce for you. And it's the same with our community."

NORTHAMPTON COMMUNITY FARM

A town protects cherished farmland, and a scrappy nonprofit pioneers a new way to support community agriculture.

WHERE: Northampton, Massachusetts

YEARS: 2009-2010

HIGHLIGHTS

• In 2009, the city of Northampton is close to acquiring the 43-acre Bean Farm and debating the land's best uses.

• The Trust for Public Land approaches the owner of the adjacent 136-acre Allard Farm about selling to the city to expand its options.

• The city asks TPL to help acquire both farms and work with a task force to determine the land's uses. State funds cover much of the combined purchase price.

• Citizens found the nonprofit Grow Food Northampton and purchase the acres reserved for farming.

SIDELIGHT

In 1842, utopian visionaries and abolitionists established a silk farm in Northampton next to what became the Bean Farm; it was a stop on the Underground Railroad.

"As a landowner, Grow Food Northampton is able to promote its nonprofit goals by offering young farmers one of the hardest things to find to get started— long-term, secure access to quality farmland."

—Clem Clay, director, TPL Connecticut River Program

where young farmers start their careers with secure long-term land leases, families stop by for local produce, and residents raise their own food in one of 400 community garden plots. And it serves as a model for other communities seeking to protect farmland and grow more of their own food closer to home.

Above: Nate Frigard and Jen Smith are leasing farmland for their Crimson & Clover Farm. Jerry and Marcy Monkman/ EcoPhotography. Below: TPL program director Clem Clay at the farm's produce distribution barn. Jerry and Marcy Monkman/EcoPhotography.

When City of Northampton announced a deal to purchase the Bean Farm, more than 40 fertile acres along the Mill River in west-central Massachusetts, it seemed everyone wanted a piece of it. Farmers and food advocates wanted to preserve the silty, well-drained soil for local food production. Open space proponents wanted to extend the Mill River Greenway and protect the river's floodplain. And the city's recreation department needed land for baseball and soccer fields.

With giant helpings of passion and energy from residents—and a big boost from The Trust for Public Land—everyone got what they wanted. The solution was to buy not one farm but two: Clem Clay, who directs TPL's Connecticut River program, and senior project manager Chris LaPointe, persuaded the owner of an adjacent 140-acre farm to sell as well. Northampton officials asked TPL to seek additional funding and help broker a consensus about the land's uses. In the end, the city bought some 60 acres for the ballfields and greenway, leaving 121 acres permanently protected for agriculture.

Grow Food Northampton, a brand-new local nonprofit, raised funds from 1,300 contributors to become the new owners of the farmland. Today the Northampton Community Farm is a place

NEW ENGLAND COMMUNITY FORESTS

"The Randolph Community Forest was the first acquired specifically for the purpose of being managed for recreation, ecological protection, and sustainable timber harvesting. TPL was a close partner and stayed with us throughout the process"

—David Willcox, town moderator, Randolph, New Hampshire

Right: Supporters display posters celebrating the Randolph Community Forest at a tenth-anniversary gathering. Jerry and Marcy Monkman/EcoPhotography. Below: Hiking in Brushwood Community Forest, West Fairlee, Vermont. Jerry and Marcy Monkman/EcoPhotography.

Northern New England communities reinterpret the colonial-era town forest to conserve the region's disappearing woodlands and open space.

WHERE: Northern New England

YEARS: 2001–present

HIGHLIGHTS

- In 2001, The Trust for Public Land helps the town of Randolph, New Hampshire, acquire 10,200 acres for a town forest, establishing a model for future projects.
- In 2007, TPL and the Community Forest Collaborative publish a report promoting community forests.
- Congress in 2008 creates a new federal grant program to fund community forests.
- To date, TPL has helped create or expand 12 community forests in northern New England.

SIDELIGHT

The Randolph Community Forest safeguards the Pond of Safety, so named because it provided a refuge for patriots during the Revolutionary War.

WHAT'S NEXT?

A planned community forest in Barre Town, Vermont, will protect former granite quarries that are now a mountain biking destination.

Tiny Randolph, New Hampshire (population 350), boasts that state's largest town forest—more than 10,000 acres of sustainably harvested timber, hiking trails, old-growth trees, and vernal pools—created by the town in 2001 with help from The Trust for Public Land. Funding for the project included money from the Federal Forest Legacy Program, established to help preserve working forests. In the years since, the forest has generated 5.5 million board feet of timber for lumber and paper pulp. Hunters, backcountry skiers, and three snowmobile clubs share the terrain. Small meadows offering spectacular views of the Presidential Range have been cleared to support breeding woodcock and migrant birds—meadows where houses would likely stand today had the land been sold for development. "Recreation and wildlife are our bottom line," said David Willcox, one of three community members who spearheaded the effort, in a 2012 *Land&People* story.

TPL's partnership with Randolph helped kick off the modern community forest movement in northern New England. Town forests are a New England tradition dating back to colonial days: towns once owned forests to supply firewood for public buildings or timber for local mills. But in the past decade communities across the region have shown how locally owned, locally controlled forestland can contain sprawl, maintain open space for recreation, protect water supplies and wildlife, and generate revenue from timber sales. As a source of timber-related jobs and income from outdoor recreation, community forests help strengthen local economies.

Interest in community forests also has been sparked by a sense of urgency about preserving the region's forested character. For the first time since forests began to reclaim farm fields in 19th century,

The northern Presidential Range of the White Mountains as seen from the Randolph Community Forest. Jerry and Marcy Monkman/EcoPhotography.

forest cover is declining in all six New England states—but this time it's pavement and houses that are replacing the trees.

"This new community forestry movement is not only focused on protecting traditional jobs in the woods ... but also includes a broader set of benefits to a community," says Rodger Krussman, TPL's Vermont and New Hampshire state director. In the last decade, the office has helped create or expand 12 community forests in the two states, totaling over 25,000 acres. Other communities where TPL has helped create community forests include Errol, Freedom, Albany, and Meredith, New Hampshire; and Hinesburg and West Fairlee, Vermont.

In 2005, TPL joined with other groups to found the Community Forest Collaborative, which worked to define a model and analyze the potential role of community forests in regional conservation strategies as well as community and economic devel-opment. The collaborative's report, *Community Forests: A Community Investment Strategy*, includes GIS analysis, interviews, surveys, input from workshops, and five case studies of community forests in northern New England.

In recent decades the community forest idea has spread from New England to communities nationwide. "The movement is really about reconnecting people with their forests," says Jad Daley, who leads TPL's community forest policy work in Washington, D.C. Daley has been helping to lead a coalition of some 130 organizations in support of the Community Forest Program, a new federal grant program administered by the U.S. Forest Service. The program makes 50-50 matching grants to towns, Indian tribes, and local land trusts to purchase land for community forests, with a focus on economic and environmental benefits, educa-tion, forest stewardship, and recreation.

GALLATIN COUNTY RANCHES

Above: Gallatin County ranchland. Alex Diekmann. *Right: Rancher Harry Armstrong and his daughter, Elizabeth, on the Half Circle Ranch, one of more than 30 ranches protected with county bond funds.* Megan Haywood-Sullivan.

"It might not work for everyone, but for those who decide to participate, it helps families keep their land in production and provides opportunities for the next generation."

—Joe Skinner, Gallatin County commissioner and the first rancher to join the county program

Funding measures designed by The Trust for Public Land's Conservation Finance experts help Gallatin County protect its Big Sky landscapes.

WHERE: Gallatin County, Montana

YEARS: 1999–2010

HIGHLIGHTS

• The rural character of a Montana valley is at risk as Gallatin County's population grows by 140 percent in 35 years.

• In 1990, citizens found the Gallatin Valley Land Trust to preserve open space, agricultural land, and wildlife habitat, and create public trails.

• In 2000 and 2004, voters approve conservation bond measures created by TPL and local partners, each for $10 million.

• To date, more than 30 ranches and farms are protected by the county's open space program with this funding—and often with TPL's help.

SIDELIGHT

To raise more funds, the Open Lands Board issues a specialty auto license plate for open space protection; by 2005 sales of the popular plate top $400,000.

From the northern rim of the Gallatin Valley you can see two Montanas. Off in the hazy distance is Bozeman, a fast-growing urban center where new subdivisions and big-box developments rule the horizon. In the foreground, across a sweep of tree-lined creek bottoms and sloping grasslands, is an inspiring alternative: thousands of acres of Big Sky country, dotted with farm and ranch buildings. Meandering tributary creeks feed the Gallatin River, a renowned trout stream. Within the valley and its foothills and forested slopes, a matrix of life zones offers habitat to hundreds of species of native flora and fauna.

Keeping this view unchanged forever has been the mission of local conservationists and groups such as the Gallatin Valley Land Trust (GVLT), founded in 1990. At first land was conserved mainly with donated conservation easements from ranchers and farmers and wealthy out-of-staters, but it became clear that some way to raise local funds for open space was needed. In 2000, The Trust for Public Land's Conservation Finance Program worked with the GVLT and the Gallatin County Commission to organize, promote, and pass the state's first county-wide open space bond measure. Another measure passed in 2004, bringing the total raised for local conservation to $20 million.

To manage the bond funds, the county appointed an Opens Lands Board, a 15-member citizens' advisory group that prioritizes and approves all open space expenditures. Often TPL helps negotiate the easements with landowners and finds funds to match the county dollars. To date, almost 40,000 acres or 62 square miles of ranches and farms have been protected under the program.

GRIGGS FARM

The Trust for Public Land helps a community protect the last farm in town from megastore development.

WHERE: Billerica, Massachusetts

YEAR: 1995

HIGHLIGHTS
- Operated by Gill Griggs since 1952, Griggs Farm sustains the agricultural heritage of Billerica.
- In 1995, the owner of 33 acres leased by Griggs agrees to sell for development of a retail superstore.
- TPL options the property to forestall the sale and negotiates a much lower purchase price for the town.
- Two-thirds of attendees at the Billerica town meeting vote to purchase the farm.

SIDELIGHT
The median income in Billerica in 1995, when citizens voted to assume a more than $1 million debt to save Griggs Farm, was $47,830.

"This is the last large farm tract in the area, and it's good productive land."

—Gill Griggs

Established in 1943, Gill Griggs's Farm was the place to go for spring tomato plants or fall pumpkins in Billerica, Massachusetts, 18 miles northwest of Boston—the last remnant of agriculture in a landscape largely swamped by sprawl development. But that farm was almost lost in 1995, when a retail superstore set its sights on 33 leased acres that Griggs's operation needed to survive.

Many Billerica residents were dismayed by the prospect of losing the town's last farm beneath acres of megastore and parking lots. Under a Massachusetts law designed to keep land in farming, Billerica itself could acquire the land if it matched the store developer's offer within 120 days—and with only three weeks to go, the town contacted The Trust for Public Land in search of options. TPL quickly discovered that the land could be acquired for about half of what the town had been told, but at more than $1 million it was still a lot of money.

Local preservationists took heart and launched a campaign to build support for the farm's protection. They held open houses at the farm, ran newspaper ads, and organized an exhibit celebrating the town's agricultural heritage. At the annual town meeting that November, 95 people stood up for open space—one vote over the two-thirds majority needed. The decision withstood a legal challenge from the developer, again with TPL's help, and Gil Griggs continued to farm the land well into his eighties. When he died in 2006, he left Billerica two important legacies: the farm (now run by his son, William), and the understanding that neighbors working together can shape the future of their communities.

Top: Farmer Gill Griggs. Susan Lapides. *Below: A farmworker harvests corn on Griggs Farm in 1995, the year Billerica residents voted to save it.* Susan Lapides.

WET MOUNTAIN VALLEY RANCHES

"Our objectives are to preserve the agricultural character and use of this land by keeping large tracts in the hands of ranching families like the Rusks, and by heading off further subdivision and development that threaten the incredible scenic and natural resources of this valley."

—Doug Robotham, former director, TPL's Colorado office

Right: A decorative gateway at the Rusk Ranch. Darcy Kiefel. Below: Musicians at a branding barbecue. Darcy Kiefel.

In a verdant Colorado Valley, The Trust for Public Land works to keep ranchers and wildlife home on the range.

WHERE: Custer County, Colorado

YEARS: 2000–2008

HIGHLIGHTS
* By the 21st century, a surge of development and rising property values in the Wet Mountain Valley add to the woes of ranchers hoping to stay on the land.
* TPL joins with local land trusts, foundation partners, and government agencies to launch the Wet Mountain Valley Ranchland Preservation Program.
* In 2003, the program acquires a conservation easement for 1,200 acres of the Rusk Hereford Ranch near Westcliffe.
* By 2008 TPL and its partners have protected more than 10,000 acres in the valley by purchasing the development rights to ranchland.

SIDELIGHT
Ranchers celebrated the 10,000-acre protection milestone with a roundup and branding barbecue.

WHAT'S NEXT?
Active ranchland protection projects in the upper Arkansas River Valley build on the success in Custer County.

"There are fewer than 35 working ranches left in Custer County," Randy Rusk told *Land&People* magazine in 2002. Ranching culture runs deep in southern Colorado's Custer County, especially in the Wet Mountain Valley, where Randy's family has owned a 1,553-acre Hereford ranch since 1946. Wedged between the Sangre de Cristo and Wet Mountains, the valley's high, lush meadows are also prime habitat for elk, pronghorn, raptors, and an unusual wealth of native plants.

But this pastoral valley lies within commuting distance of southern Colorado's fast-growing cities and has been a magnet for residential and vacation-home developers. Ranchettes now line the southern border of the Rusk family's ranch; front lawns and flower beds have replaced pastures where cattle once grazed.

As elsewhere in the mountain West, the deck is stacked against ranchers who don't want to sell or subdivide their lands. They face high operating costs, low beef prices, inheritance taxes based on the developed value of agricultural real estate, children who seek a different kind of life. Yet many would keep on ranching if they could—and The Trust for Public Land has come to their aid, helping them protect their land through the purchase of development rights (PDR). This type of conservation easement can lower ranchers' tax liability, raise enough money to keep them in business, and preserve the land from uses that threaten natural resources and traditional, land-based livelihoods. In 2001, TPL joined with the National Cattlemen's Beef Association and the Western Governors' Association to produce a report on the potential of PDR as a tool to protect ranchland, *Purchase of Development Rights: Conserving Lands, Preserving Western Livelihoods.*

Important support for the effort in Colorado has come from Great Outdoors Colorado (GOCO), a conservation funding program that uses part of the proceeds from the state's lottery. Between 2000 and 2008, TPL worked with GOCO, local nonprofits, foundations, and ranching families like the Rusks to protect more than 10,000 acres in the Wet Mountain Valley. TPL's role has been to structure transactions that best serve the needs of the community, the rancher, and the land itself; facilitate fundraising; and work with all concerned parties to develop a conservation-oriented management plan. In the case of the Rusk ranch, this work took nearly three years.

The easement is now held by the Colorado Cattlemen's Agricultural Land Trust (CCALT), so that the ranch can never be developed.

"It's been worth all the time because it will help ensure the future of this ranch and ranching in general in Custer County," Randy Rusk told *Land & People* magazine in 2004. In addition to its work in the Wet Mountain Valley, TPL has used easements to protect Colorado ranches in the Gunnison Valley, the Yampa Valley, the San Luis Valley, and the valley of the upper Arkansas River.

For the ranchers, the financial benefits of selling development rights may make it possible for them to protect their land. But their real motivation springs from their devotion to ranching, which transcends economics. It's a way of ensuring that they can continue to earn a living on the land—and so can their grandkids.

Calves are rounded up for branding at the Rusk Ranch. Between 2000 and 2008, TPL and its partners protected more than 10,000 acres of ranchland in the Wet Mountain Valley. Darcy Kiefel.

About The Trust for Public Land

THE TRUST FOR PUBLIC LAND conserves land for people to enjoy as parks, gardens, and other natural places, ensuring livable communities for generations to come.

Working from more than 30 offices nationwide, the trust offers a range of services to address the conservation needs of the 21st century. We help communities plan for growth, raise funds, acquire land, and renovate parks and playgrounds; and we conduct research to support parks and conservation.

The Trust for Public Land works to protect the places people care about and to create close-to-home parks, particularly in and near cities. Our goal is that every American—especially every child—have easy access to health-building places to play. We also conserve working farms, ranches, and forests; lands of historical and cultural importance; rivers, streams, coasts, watersheds, and wildlands—lands where all Americans can experience nature close at hand.

Since 1972, The Trust for Public Land has completed more than 5,200 park and conservation projects, conserved more than 3 million acres, and helped generate more than $33 billion in state and local conservation funding—all made possible by the generosity of our donors.

For more information, to donate, to sign up for free electronic newsletters, to download publications, or to request a free copy of *Land&People* magazine, please visit tpl.org.

Acknowledgments

The Trust for Public Land and the creators of this book are grateful to Timothy Egan for contributing the perfect foreword. We are also indebted to all those members of the organization's staff and volunteer leadership—past and present—who contributed so much to its portrait in these pages. They include: Ralph Benson, Margie Kim Bermeo, Nancy Biskovich, Shirley Chambers, Ernest Cook, Jad Daley, Jay Dean, Kathy DeCoster, George Denny, Douglas P. Ferguson, Bob Flewelling, Jennie Gerard, Yasaman Golban, Peter Harnik, Holly Haugh, James S. Hoyte, Karen MacDonald, Brenda McClymonds, Scott Parker, Breece Robertson, Jessica Sargent-Michaud, Will Rogers, Martin J. Rosen, Alia Salim, Eliza Sarasohn, Helene Sherlock, Andy Stone, Jerry Tone, Rand Wentworth, and Martha Wyckoff.

We acknowledge as well the professional assistance of proofreader David Sweet, indexer Elizabeth Parson, and the pre-media staff of Quad/Graphics in San Francisco.

P.S. 181, New York City. Larry Bercow.

Index of Places and Projects

Land for People was designed by Linda Herman/Glyph Publishing Arts, based on concepts by Shirley Chambers. The text is set in Spectrum with Rotis san serif heads. Quad/Graphics Media Solutions of San Francisco provided image work and retouching, and the book was printed and bound by Taylor Specialty Books in Dallas, Texas. The text stock is 80-pound Sterling Dull Book Recycled, and the endpapers are printed on 90-pound Springhill Index Recycled. The case is bound in Rainbow Brillianta cloth manufactured by Van Heek Textiles. Photograph on this page: *Gaviota Coast, California*. Rich Reid Photography.com.

Bee Canyon, Los Angeles, 1973 ✦ Richfield Coliseum, Ohio, 1999 ✦ Happles Lake, Wisconsin, 2001 ✦ Neponset Greenway, Massachusetts, 2002 ✦ Marian Fathers Ballfields, Chicago, 2003 ✦ Elkhorn Ranch, Utah, 2004 ✦ 13 Mile Woods, New Hampshire, 2005 ✦ Pochuck Mountain, New York, 2006 ✦ Martin Luther King Jr. Historic Site, Georgia, 1982–2010 ✦ Rum River, Minnesota, 2010 ✦ Walden Woods, Massachusetts, 1991–1994 ✦ Gallatin County Funding Measure, Montana, 2000 ✦ Highland Farm, Maine, 2009 ✦ Litchfield Hills Greenprint, Connecticut, 2005 ✦ Great White Heron National Wildlife Refuge, Florida, 1976 ✦ Lindbergh Lake, Montana, 2000 ✦ Chief Joseph Ranch, Oregon, 1999 ✦ Sawtooth National Recreation Area, 1975–1985 ✦ Tres Pistolas, New Mexico, 1998 ✦ Saint Columba Playground, Newark, 1995 ✦ Koshland Park, San Francisco, 1974 ✦ Los Angeles State Historic Park, 2001 ✦ Clinton Community Garden, New York, 1985 ✦ Olympic Sculpture Park, Seattle, 1999 ✦ P.S. 176 Playground, Brooklyn, 2010 ✦ Woonasquatucket River Greenway, Rhode Island, 2007 ✦ Cuyahoga Valley National Park, Ohio, 1978–2011 ✦ Signal Bay Park, Texas, 1989 ✦ Buffalo Hill Farm, Massachusetts, 2012 ✦ Webb Mountain Park, Connecticut, 2004 ✦ Northside District Park, Tucson, 1987 ✦ Kawa Bay, Hawai'i, 2011 ✦ Golden Gate Canyon State Park, Colorado, 1989 ✦ Gwynns Falls Trail, Baltimore, 1992–2005 ✦ Ruffner Mountain, Alabama, 1983 ✦ Case Park, Tucson, 1987 ✦ Turnbull Hammock, Florida, 1980 ✦ Atascadero Creek, California, 2011 ✦ P.S. 180 Playground, Harlem, 2006 ✦ Peace River Park, Florida, 1978 ✦ Central Texas Greenprint, 2009 ✦ Dog Mountain, Washington, 1985 ✦ Hutchinson Ranch, Colorado, 2011 ✦ New York Community Gardens, 1978–2012 ✦ Sutton Creek, Oregon, 1986 ✦ Bruce Vento Nature Sanctuary, Saint Paul, 2007–2008 ✦ Broad Canyon Ranch, New Mexico, 2009 ✦ Bluebird Ranch, California, 2008 ✦ St. George Island State Park, Florida, 1984 ✦ Sentinel Peak Park, Tucson, 1990 ✦ Tilly Foster Farm, New York, 2002 ✦ O'Melveny Park, Los Angeles, 1973 ✦ Mallows Bay, Maryland, 2002 ✦ Cahuenga Peak, Los Angeles, 2012 ✦ Ash Lake, Minnesota, 1993 ✦ City Park, New Orleans, 2009 ✦ Visitacion Valley Greenway, San Francisco, 1999–2004 ✦ Ramapo Mountains County Park, New Jersey, 1989 ✦ Gray's Harbor County Park, Washington, 1986 ✦ York River State Park, Virginia, 2003 ✦ Harper's Ferry National Historic Park, West Virginia, 2002 ✦ Cape Romano, Florida, 1975 ✦ Mitchell Lakes, Colorado, 2012 ✦ National Bison Range, Montana, 1987 ✦ Overtown Playground, Miami, 2002 ✦ Phillips Farm, Virginia, 2003 ✦ Ruckel Creek, Oregon, 1987 ✦ Trinity Rec Fitness Zone, South Los Angeles, 2010 ✦ Barnegat Bay, New Jersey, 1983–2012 ✦ Oakland Bay, Washington, 2012 ✦ Bear Creek Canyon, Colorado, 1992 ✦ Potso Dog Park, Oregon, 2011 ✦ Chickasaw National Recreation Area, Oklahoma, 1991 ✦ Decker Farm, New York, 2003 ✦ Temecula Mountain, California,

2011 ◆ East River Greenprint, New York, 2003 ◆ Point Lookout State Park, Maryland, 1992 ◆ Nassau County Funding

1987 ◆ Santa Venetia County Park, California, 1974 ◆ Westside Community Garden, New York, 1989 ◆ Sue Creek Park,

1991 ◆ Pine Avenue Park, Los Angeles, 2011 ◆ Weir Farm National Historic Site, Connecticut, 1990 ◆ East Everglades, F

Franklin D. Roosevelt National Historic Site, New York, 1989 ◆ General Morris Forest, New York, 2006 ◆ Columbia River Gorge

Mountain Island Lake, North Carolina, 1998–2009 ◆ Otterbrook, New York, 1991 ◆ Matchett Farm, Colorado, 1996 ◆ Gar

Lake, New York, 2004 ◆ Wilkins Ranch, California, 1973 ◆ Lake Oconee, Georgia, 1982 ◆ World Thoreau Center, Mass

Long Island, Minnesota, 2007 ◆ Arrowhead Farm, Massachusetts, 1993 ◆ Last Chance Pond, New York, 2004 ◆ Chero

2001 ◆ Oregon Caves, Oregon, 1979 ◆ Jug Bay Farm, Maryland, 2004 ◆ Big Island Lake, Minnesota, 1989 ◆ Los Liones Can

◆ Dog Creek Falls, Washington, 1985 ◆ Wonder Lake, New York, 2006 ◆ Hoboken Riverfront Park, New Jersey, 2006 ◆ Wh

San Francisco, 1986 ◆ Knobs State Forest, Kentucky, 2006 ◆ Miller Island, Washington, 1989 ◆ Sheridan Point, Orego

2007 ◆ Royal River Estuary, Maine, 2004 ◆ Minneapolis Community Gardens, 2003 ◆ Bald Hill, Connecticut, 1988

Ridge, New York, 2004 ◆ Cove Hollow Farm, New York, 1993 ◆ Breezy Point, Maryland, 1995 ◆ Woodland Creek, Was

1988 ◆ Foster Farm, New York, 1995 ◆ Rocky Creek, Texas, 1994 ◆ Phenn Basin, Vermont, 1997 ◆ Bufflehead Bay, Ma

1994 ◆ Jewell Wetlands, Colorado, 1995 ◆ Hillside Woods, New York, 1993 ◆ Cathedral of Pines, Wisconsin, 1990 ◆ Sci

Creek, Oregon, 2010 ◆ Forges Field, Massachusetts, 1993 ◆ Hall Ranch, Colorado, 1996 ◆ Buzzard Rock, West Virgin

1992 ◆ Lawton Park, Washington, 1996 ◆ Monticello Fields, Ohio, 1991 ◆ Olmstead View, Oregon, 1998 ◆ Portland W

Ranch, Colorado, 1996 ◆ Witch Hollow Farm, Massachusetts, 1995 ◆ Rush Island, Minnesota, 1991 ◆ McKay Park, O

2005 ◆ Dagnon Ranch, Washington, 2010 ◆ Homer Spit, Alaska, 1998 ◆ Rye Creek, Montana, 2005 ◆ Big Lake, Wash

2004 ◆ Salt River, Virgin Islands, 2004 ◆ Badger Mountain, Washington, 2005 ◆ Biddle Butte, Washington, 1988 ◆ Ser

Ghost Lake, Wisconsin, 1992 ◆ Three Rivers, Arkansas, 2003 ◆ Snow Mountain Ranch, Washington, 2005 ◆ Gilgal

Oregon, 2000 ◆ Cowling Creek, Washington, 2003 ◆ Moffitt Hollow, Vermont, 1993 ◆ Caribbean Gardens, Florida, 20

Landing, Florida, 2008 ◆ Laidlaw, Oregon, 2008 ◆ Montana Legacy, 1997–2010 ◆ Phelps Creek, Washington, 1997 ◆ Hall

Connecticut, 2005 ◆ Reeds Creek Farm, Illinois, 1993 ◆ Halifax River Park, Florida, 2009 ◆ Lake of the Woods, Mic

Hampshire, 2009 ◆ Sipican Harbor, Massachusetts, 1996 ◆ Duck Creek Wetlands, Montana, 2004 ◆ Sugarloaf Key,

2005 ◆ Windrush Farm, Massachusetts, 2009 ◆ Gold Star Farm, New Hampshire, 2005 ◆ Bull Creek Fish Camp, F

Ranch, California, 2001 ◆ Awosting Preserve, New York, 2006 ◆ Mt. Gilboa, Massachusetts, 1990 ◆ Meserve Farm